Le
TOUR
de FRANCE

LE TOUR DE FRANCE

Summersdale Publishers Ltd
46 West Street
Chichester
West Sussex
PO19 1RP
UK

www.summersdale.com

Printed and bound by CPI Group (UK) Ltd, Crydon, CR0 4YY

ISBN: 978-1-84953-507-6

Substantial discounts on bulk quantities of Summersdale books are available to corporations, professional associations and other organisations. For details contact Nicky Douglas by telephone: +44 (0) 1243 756902, fax: +44 (0) 1243 786300 or email: nicky@summersdale.com.

Le
TOUR
de FRANCE

The Greatest
Race in Cycling
History

Ray Hamilton

For Holly

Contents

Introduction

The Tour de France is the most famous, most anticipated and most exciting bicycle race in the world. It takes place annually over a three-week period across the roads of (mostly) France in a great, loosely fashioned loop through cities, towns and villages, along coasts and lakesides, across hills and mountains, and through a bewildering variety of rural landscapes. For good measure, the organisers provide by way of backdrop as many World Heritage Sites and *châteaux* as they can cram into the route, which in itself is never the same from one year to the next. It is, in short, everything the French Tourist Board could possibly wish it to be.

As elaborate as that might sound, though, it barely scratches the surface. To really get up close and personal with the Tour, you need to look beyond its impressive size and scale and familiarise yourself with over a hundred years of history; with the complexity of the competitions within the competition; with the levels of fitness, speed and endurance attained by its superhuman participants; with the perpetual technological advances of the bikes and all the other equipment (even if riders do still stuff newspapers down their jerseys to stay warm on mountain downhills);

with the massive scale of the logistical operations that underpin the race; with the quite dizzying media hype that swarms around its successes, failures and scandals; with the ever-increasing amounts of corporate advertising and sponsorship; with the French people's (justifiable) obsession with everything and anything to do with 'their' Tour; and with the extreme passion and interest which the race arouses in its millions of followers and spectators around the world.

This book attempts to capture all of that in a manner that is easy to digest and which will give clear insights into the many things that are going on at any one time during the race, both for those who are relatively new to the subject and for those who, like me, are already obsessed by the Tour de France and all its ups and downs.

And, yes, Lance Armstrong does get mentioned a few times.

Note: All results, records and statistics in this book are, to the best of my knowledge, correct as at the end of March 2013.

Chapter 1
La Grande Boucle

'As a test of physical and mental endurance, it has no equal... It's the only race in the world where you have to get a haircut halfway through.'

Chris Boardman, three-times Tour stage winner

The Tour de France is one of three 'Grand Tours', the other two being the Giro d'Italia and the Vuelta a España, but the Tour de France is the one that most cyclists dream of taking part in or, even better, completing. For the top riders, it is the one they most want on their so-called *palmarès* (the list of their cycling triumphs). It is to cycling what Wimbledon is to tennis, what the Grand National is to horse racing, what the Super Bowl is to American football. Along with the Giro and the Road World Cycling Championship, the Tour de France also makes up the Triple Crown of cycling each year. (This has only ever been won twice, by Eddy

Merckx of Belgium in 1974 and by Stephen Roche of Ireland in 1987.) The Tour is also a component part of the UCI (Union Cycliste Internationale) World Tour, which maintains the world ranking system for professional cyclists.

The French often refer to their Tour as 'La Grande Boucle' – The Big Loop (literally 'buckle') – because that's exactly what it was originally, a race around the circumference of France (see 'Around France' in the chapter headed 'The Race' for more detail).

The Father of the Tour

Henri Desgrange was the (initially reluctant) father of the Tour de France and, as such, the inventor of the sport of bicycle stage racing. A prominent track cyclist and velodrome owner at the turn of the twentieth century, he was appointed editor of the fledgling sports newspaper *L'Auto-Vélo* in 1900. After a court ruling in 1903 decreed that the paper's name was too close to that of its fierce rival *Le Vélo*, the name was shortened to just *L'Auto* and the pages became yellow in contrast to the green of *Le Vélo*. *L'Auto* would later morph into *L'Équipe* after World War Two.

Convinced by others in 1903 that sponsorship of a cycling road race around France would boost sales, the Tour was born, although Desgrange took no real part in its organisation. Surprised by its success, he took a more hands-on approach to the second Tour the following year, only to be dismayed by the disqualification of the first four riders home (because they had been towed by cars or had jumped on buses or trains during the night-time periods of the race!). But he overcame his early doubts to take almost dictatorial control of the race for the next thirty years. The harsh rules and penalties he imposed on riders made him unpopular, but the race was exactly what he wanted it to be – a real test of strength and endurance for men of steel.

Full Moon

Desgrange's legacy is a race that is still being run in the twenty-first century. If you had set out in the direction of the moon in 1903 to cycle the combined distance of all the Tour routes that have been run since then, you would be on your way back now.

'The men waved their hats, the ladies their umbrellas. One felt they would have liked to touch the steel muscles of the most courageous champions since antiquity.'

**L'Auto, 1 July 1903
(reporting on the start of the first Tour)**

When is a Centenary Not a Centenary?

It took the Tour de France 110 years to reach its centenary race in 2013 because of the years lost to the two world wars. The race did take place in 1914, the starter pistol having been fired the same morning as the pistol shot that killed Archduke Ferdinand of Austria in Sarajevo and precipitated World War One. The next Tour was after the war in 1919.

The 1939 Tour took place a few weeks before the outbreak of World War Two but without teams from Germany, Italy or Spain, as animosity across Europe had long since reached heights that prevented sporting camaraderie. The race would not be run again until 1947 in spite of German pressure to run the race during the war years in order to maintain a semblance of normality in occupied France.

Race Composition

Although the early Tours were limited to a straightforward race around the periphery of France, a number of changes over the years have resulted in the multifaceted competition we enjoy today. The composition of the twenty-one stages that now comprise the Tour varies from year to year. It will typically include a couple of individual time trials (where each rider races alone against the clock) and a team time trial (where each nine-man team races on its own against the clock). The remainder will be so-called 'mass-start stages', which will either be flat (primarily for the sprinters to show what they're made of), hilly (ideal for breakaways) or mountainous (where the climbers get to slug it out).

Individual time trials were first introduced in 1934 and are sometimes used as a 'prologue' to the race on day one. The first such prologue took place in 1967 at Angers, and the one that took place in London in 2007 (along with the London to Canterbury stage the following day) gripped the British nation with a Tour fever that shows no sign of abating. Team time trials had been introduced in 1927, when the twenty-four-stage Tour consisted of sixteen team time trials, five mountain stages and only three 'plain stages' for individual riders on the flat. Time trials, in common with other stage wins, help to boost overall earnings as they bring in around €10,000 for a team or individual win.

General Classification (GC) (Classement Général)

Much more commonly known as the Yellow Jersey (Maillot Jaune) competition, this is the ultimate prize in cycling, awarded to the rider who completes the overall Tour de France course in the shortest time. Generally speaking, if you're going to win the GC, you're going to have to be a very strong climber, a more-than-decent time triallist and a rider who can stay out of trouble in the pack on the flatter stages while the sprinters ahead are going for glory. To stay in contention, or maintain the lead that you gained in a previous stage or stages, it is often enough to cross the line in the middle of the main bunch (the so-called '*peloton*') as those riders are all awarded the same finishing time (so you do have to be sure that your main rivals are in the same peloton and not speeding ahead in an individual or group breakaway).

After day one, the yellow jersey is worn each day by the overall race leader. In the early years of the race, the leader wore a green armband, but this wasn't obvious enough to other riders, spectators or officials, so by 1919 the armband had been replaced by the more identifiable yellow jersey. Desgrange chose yellow because, as we have seen, that was the colour of his *L'Auto* newspaper pages.

From a total Tour 'prize pot' of over €2 million, the pot for the Yellow Jersey competition alone is around €1 million. The Yellow Jersey winner pockets around €500,000 of that, with the runner-up getting around €200,000, third place around €100,000, and so on all the way down to a few hundred euros for finishing outside the first ninety riders home. The prize money awarded in 1903 to chimney sweep Maurice Garin for winning the first Tour was 12,000 francs, roughly £18,000 in today's terms but still about six times what most workers could earn in a year in the early twentieth century. Occasionally over the years sponsors have thrown in extra incentives and the Belgian Lucien van Impe received an apartment in addition to his prize money for winning the 1976 Tour.

Points Classification (Classement par Points)

More commonly known as the Green Jersey (Maillot Vert) competition, this is the competition for the fastest riders, or sprinters. The competition was introduced in 1953 to mark the fiftieth anniversary of the first Tour and the colour green was chosen because the original sponsor was the lawnmower manufacturer La Belle Jardinière. Points are awarded for stage wins, for intermediate sprints within stages, and for the fastest times recorded in individual and team time trials. Each day the competition leader gets to wear the green jersey, but to win the Green Jersey competition overall, the rider also needs to reach Paris at the end of the Tour, easier said than done when your training regime is not primarily designed to get you over tough mountain climbs. The sprinter who does eventually race up the Champs-Elysées with the most points in his saddlebag stands to make around €25,000 plus around €8,000 for each stage win and around €1,000 for each sprint win.

In The Pink

The equivalent of the yellow jersey in the Giro d'Italia is the pink jersey (*maglia rosa*), and it is pink for exactly the same reason that the yellow jersey of the Tour de France is yellow i.e. because the Giro is organised by the Italian newspaper *La Gazzetta dello Sport*, the pages of which are – you guessed it – pink.

King of the Mountains (Classement des Grimpeurs)

The best climber (*meilleur grimpeur*) of the Tour has been recognised since the early years of the competition, with prizes awarded since 1934. The points system used today awards points to the first riders over the top of each climb – the more difficult the climb, the more points awarded, with double points awarded for the final climb of the day. The highest points are awarded for reaching the summits of legendary climbs such as the Col du Tourmalet, Mont Ventoux and l'Alpe d'Huez, which are considered so difficult that they are classified as *hors catégorie* (beyond categorisation). The leader, and the ultimate winner, of the King of the Mountains competition wears a white jersey with red polka dots (*maillot à pois rouges*), because the first sponsor in 1934 was Chocolat Poulain, the manufacturer of a chocolate bar that had a polka dot wrapper. The climber who makes it back to earth with the most points stands to make around €25,000 plus around €8,000 for each stage win and around €1,000 for each climb win.

Tour de Crufts

In 2009 Alberto Contador may or may not have been thrilled when he also received a slobbering St Bernard dog for winning the mountain stage up in the Swiss Alps.

Best Young Rider (Classement des Jeunes)

Also known as the White Jersey (Maillot Blanc) competition, this is no different to the Yellow Jersey competition, except that it is confined to riders under the age of twenty-six. The prize was first awarded in 1975 and was officially renamed the Souvenir Fabio Casartelli in 1997, in memory of the Italian rider who lost his life after crashing on a descent in the Pyrenees in 1995. The overall best young rider will net around €25,000 plus around €500 each time he records the best time in a stage in the Young Rider category.

Miscellaneous Jerseys

In addition to those riders wearing the official Tour jerseys described above, it is not uncommon to see others wearing 'non-regulation' jerseys instead of their team colours. These riders will be national champions sporting the colours of their home nation or, in the case of a 'rainbow jersey', the current road-race or time-trial world champion.

Most Aggressive Rider (Prix de la Combativité)

In spite of the prize's name, no points are awarded for kicking, punching, spitting or gouging. Instead, the Prix de la Combativité has been awarded since 1952 to the rider in each stage who makes the most or the strongest attacking moves, which often take the form of breakaways from the peloton. In addition to the cash prize on offer, the winner gets to wear a symbolic white-on-red (instead of black-on-white) identification number in the next stage. Based on a points system, the overall winner *(le super-combatif)* at the end of the Tour will net around €20,000 plus around €2,000 for each 'most aggressive' stage win.

Team Classification (Classement des Equipes)

Although many different time and points systems have been employed over the years, since 2011 this classification is determined after each stage by adding the times of the first three riders home from each team of nine, except in team time trials when the time of the fifth rider home is what gets counted. A good team performance can ensure entry to the following year's Tour, and winning the competition also brings in around €50,000 (plus around €3,000 for each stage win). See the chapter headed 'Team Spirit' for more information on this aspect of the race and its history over the years.

Ex-jerseys

Until 1989 there was a Red Jersey competition for the fastest riders in the intermediate sprints within stages. In addition to points, these riders could win cash prizes donated by the residents of the areas in which the sprints took place.

Another ex-jersey is the Combination Jersey, a patchwork design incorporating the colours of the four main jerseys based on a rider's combined standings in the Yellow, Green, Red and Polka Dot Jersey competitions. This was also abolished in 1989, robbing spectators forever of the sight of the best all-round rider of the Tour whizzing past in the worst all-round jersey of the Tour. There are no prizes for guessing that Eddy Merckx won the Combination Jersey more times than anyone else, but it is not clear whether he chose to wear it in preference to the yellow jersey he was also entitled to wear most of the time (I seriously doubt it, though).

Chapter 2
Road Warriors

'When I feel bad, I attack – that way no one can find out how bad I feel.'

Bernard Hinault, five-times Tour winner

Many different types of bike rider participate each year in the Tour de France. Occasionally history has produced a versatile all-rounder, like Eddy Merckx (Belgium) or Bernard Hinault (France), who could climb, sprint and time-trial. These all-rounders are considered the most worthy winners of the most worthy bike race on the planet, but sprinting has become such a specialism that we are unlikely to see their like again.

There are specialist time-triallists, who gain time over their rivals against the clock – if they are strong enough, like Jacques Anquetil (France) and Miguel Indurain (Spain), they can win the Tour by hanging on during the mountain stages to the time margins they built up *contre-la-montre* (against the clock) back at ground level. This was the tactic employed by Bradley Wiggins when he became the first British winner of the Tour in 2012.

There are specialist climbers, like Richard Virenque (France), Federico Bahamontes (Spain) and Lucien van Impe (Belgium). It is certainly not unknown for such climbers to win the Tour outright (although Virenque never did) because Tours are often won and lost in the mountains. But most climbers are unlikely to win anywhere but in the mountains, where their generally smaller physique (and, therefore, lower weight) allows them to perform more efficiently than heavier riders. It is not, however, uncommon for those lightweight climbers to be among the poorest descenders and to lose the time advantage gained on a climb by the time they reach the bottom again. The riders generally considered to be the top climbers of recent years are Andy Schleck (Luxembourg) and Alberto Contador (Spain).

Then, of course, there are the sprinters, the ones who excite the crowds by racing towards the finishing line in a blur of speed. It is said that sprinters are born, not made: you need a high proportion of 'fast-twitch' muscle and steely nerve to go shoulder-to-shoulder with a dozen similarly gifted riders at blistering speed. The best of them get to enjoy the glory of stage wins, arms aloft in their own inimitable styles as they cross the line, but they are the riders most unlikely to win the GC because they train for speed rather than endurance. Eddy Merckx was a notable exception to that rule, but even he is being left far behind by Britain's Mark Cavendish when it comes to sprint-finish wins in the Tour de France.

So-called breakaway riders add to the excitement of many a stage as they try, individually or as small groups, to outwit the main pack. Pedalling at or near their limits of endurance, they try to forge a lead that might just result in an unexpected stage win, or at the very least delight their sponsors on account of the air-time they enjoy on TV screens around the globe while they are out in front. Sometimes it pays off and the glory is theirs for a day. But most times the super-efficient peloton reels them back in and spits them out the back in a matter of seconds, often agonisingly close to the realisation of their dreams of glory.

Just One More Cornetto!

The Spaniard Federico Bahamontes was one of the great climbers, but was so afraid of descending on his own that he would wait at the top of a col for other riders to arrive before continuing down the mountain! He once spent several minutes eating ice cream by the side of the road until the others caught up. Such was his lack of confidence cornering on the way down that he would take one foot off the pedal to balance himself in the style of a speedway rider. Notwithstanding all of this, he still won the Yellow Jersey in 1959 and the King of the Mountains Classification six times.

*'If you go, you can either win or not win.
If you don't go, you definitely won't win.'*

**Jens Voigt, two-times Tour stage winner,
on his philosophy regarding breakaways**

And let us not forget the team players, the *domestiques*, who unselfishly give all that they have for the good of the team, or for the good of the team member who is most likely to win one or more of the big prizes. Perhaps surprisingly, these team players are not always the journeymen of bike racing – in 2012 Mark Cavendish sacrificed any chance he had of winning back-to-back Green Jersey competitions, and Chris Froome sacrificed his own chances of winning the Yellow Jersey competition, to ensure that their fellow countryman, Bradley Wiggins, became the first British rider to wear yellow atop the podium on the Champs-Elysées. Nowadays, even the sprinters rarely achieve their wins alone, relying instead on the shelter and slipstream provided by their lead-out trains, gutsy riders who set the pace and drop off the front one by one until the final lead-out man delivers the star sprinter to the front at exactly the right moment to complete the job in hand.

The Early Riders

The early Tours were open to pretty much anybody who wanted to compete, or who at least could afford the entry fee. Many rode for teams unofficially supported by bike manufacturers (the Tour organisers did not allow it on an official basis until 1962) but private entrants were allowed as long as they made no demands on the organisers. Some of those private entrants would perform acrobatics in the streets after the day's race in order to raise enough money for that night's hotel. Those early semi-professional and amateur riders didn't have to worry too much about tactics or about shaving a few seconds off their times with the latest aerodynamic gear; they simply had to pedal heavy bikes for all they were worth over unprepared terrain for impossibly long distances. They were expected to spend inhumane periods of time in the saddle – up to twenty hours to cover almost five hundred kilometres (three hundred miles) – and it was little wonder that they drank alcohol during the race to kill the inevitable pain, or that they used cars, buses or trains when nobody was looking. They had to mend their own punctures or endure severe penalties for accepting help, and they were only allowed to eat when they were allowed to eat. Little wonder, then, that the Tour captured the public imagination, but no small wonder perhaps that the early riders kept coming back for more and more punishment.

The first couple of decades of the Tour did not enjoy the international smorgasbord of riders that we see today. In fact, French riders won eight of the first nine races, interrupted only by François Faber of Luxembourg when he became the first foreigner to win the Tour in 1909. Belgian riders then helped themselves to seven consecutive Tour wins in the years spanning World War One. Lucien Petit-Breton (France) was the first man to win two Tours (1907, 1908) and Philippe Thys (Belgium) was the first man to win three (1913, 1914, 1920). Thys might have won more had it not been for the small inconvenience of the intervening war. In 1924 Ottavio Bottecchia became the first Italian to win the Tour (and the first man to wear the yellow jersey from start to finish of the race), repeating the feat in 1925. Another Italian, Gino Bartali, won in 1938 and 1948 and, like Philippe Thys exactly one world war earlier, may have won more had the venue not been turned into a large number of battlefields.

Just Like That!

Incroyable!

The first African rider to compete in the Tour was the Tunisian Ali Neffati in 1913. Also the youngest rider (at just eighteen) to have ridden the Tour at the time, he became the darling of the crowd as he cycled past them in his fez.

MAURICE GARIN

Born: Aosta, Italy, 23 March 1871
Died: Lens, France, 18 February 1957
Tour palmarès: General Classification 1903
(including three stage wins)
Nicknames: the Little Chimney Sweep; the
White Bulldog

Born in French-speaking Aosta just over the border in Italy, the diminutive Maurice Garin left the Alps behind to sweep the chimneys of northern France. He turned to bike racing after the secretary of a local cycling club spotted his potential. He won the Paris-Roubaix Classic twice, as well as some notable one-day races, before securing immortality as the first winner of the Tour de France in 1903, including the first-ever stage, from Paris to Lyon. One of his nicknames, the White Bulldog, came about as a result of the white jacket he always wore while racing.

He added notoriety to immortality when he was stripped of the 1904 title for cheating, including, as we have seen, hopping aboard public transport during the night-time periods of the race. Garin had won the 1903 race by 2 hours 49 minutes and 45 seconds, which remains to this day the highest winning margin in the Tour's history, and which does make you kind of wonder whether he had familiarised himself with the bus and train timetables of France even before the 1903 race.

Approaching the Modern Era

As the Tour approached the 'modern era' in the late 1940s and early 1950s, the Italian Fausto Coppi slugged it out with his compatriot, the aforementioned Gino Bartali, eventually forging ahead to win two Yellow Jerseys of his own (1949, 1952). As a larger-than-life character, Coppi probably also changed forever the way in which Tour riders would be viewed by the outside world (see 'Cycling's First Celebrity' below).

Fausto Coppi – Cycling's First Celebrity

Widely regarded as the sport's first 'celebrity', the Italian Fausto Coppi was a legend for all the right reasons and for quite a few wrong reasons to boot. On the road, he was an elegant and popular all-rounder who won the Tour twice. He overcame poor health as a child and a long list of training and racing injuries to climb, sprint and time-trial with the best of them. He won the 1952 Tour 28 minutes ahead of the field and took five stage wins in the process, including the Tour's first-ever summit finish at the now legendary l'Alpe d'Huez. Coppi's life off the road was equally colourful: taken prisoner-of-war by the British in North Africa; convicted of adultery (still a criminal offence at the time) after scandalising Italian society with a very public extramarital affair; and suffering a premature death, aged just 40 years old, after contracting malaria following an exhibition race in Upper Volta (now Burkina Faso).

Gino Bartali – the Vatican's Favourite

The Tuscan rider's victories either side of World War Two, ten years apart in 1938 and 1948, were achieved with the longest gap ever between Tour victories. His feat of winning three consecutive mountain stages in 1948 has also never been equalled (except by Lance Armstrong, which no longer counts). As mentioned above, his career overlapped with that of his fellow countryman Fausto Coppi. They both won the Tour twice and they were both great climbers, thrilling the crowds with their many head-to-head battles over the mountains. But there the similarities ended. Coppi and Bartali split Italian public opinion wide open. You were either a *tifoso* (fan) of the scandalous playboy Coppi (the George Best of his day), or you admired 'Gino il Pio' (Gino the Pious), as Bartali was known on account of his strong religious beliefs. There was little doubt which side the Vatican was on. Pope Pius XII blessed Bartali's wedding and received a bicycle from Bartali in return. Bartali then taught Pope John XXIII to ride, but it isn't clear whether that happened on Pius XII's bike or not.

'Don't touch him! He's a god.'

General Antonelli, Mussolini's Sports Minister, trying to keep the crowds away from Gino Bartali after he won the 1938 Tour

The Cowboy

The Swiss rider 'Ferdi' Kübler, winner of the 1950 Tour, was known as 'the Cowboy' on account of the stetsons he often wore. He was a high-spirited and impulsive rider, given to strategically unwise attacks out of sheer exuberance and competitive drive. Following a bout of over-exuberance on Mont Ventoux during the 1955 Tour, he overdid things to the extent that he was forced to pull over at a roadside cafe. To the surprise of the cafe's customers, he shouted out 'Stand clear, Ferdi about to explode!' before jumping back on his bike and heading off in the wrong direction.

Brit Abroad

In 1955 Brian Robinson from Huddersfield became the first British rider to complete the Tour de France. He then became the first Brit to win a stage when he won a bunch sprint into Brest in 1958, and proved it was no fluke the following year when he broke away from the peloton to win a stage by 20 minutes.

The Modern Era

The 1950s saw the first of what would ultimately be five victories for France's Jacques Anquetil (achieved between 1957 and 1964), and produced the first Spanish winner of the Tour, Federico Bahamontes, in 1959.

The introduction of the Points Classification for sprinters in 1953 changed the face of the Tour forever. From that moment on, an even greater variety of riders would be on show, as sprinters took their place alongside climbers, time triallists and the supermen of the sport, the all-rounders. Let us first take a look at the supermen.

The Supermen

With Jacques Anquetil rewriting the record books in the swinging sixties, we had arrived in the modern age of the supermen. A total of four riders have since won the Tour de France five times, Anquetil having been followed by the Belgian Eddy Merckx (between 1969 and 1974), then a second Frenchman, Bernard Hinault (between 1978 and 1985), and then the Spaniard Miguel Indurain, the first man to win five consecutive Tours (between 1991 and 1995). The American Lance Armstrong surpassed them all with seven consecutive wins between 1999 and 2005, but all seven victories have since been consigned to the dustbin, reducing the Big Five of cycling to the Big Four, and leaving American Greg LeMond, with three wins, as the most successful non-European in the race's history. Bernard

Hinault was the last French winner of the Yellow Jersey in 1985 – if you're French, this hurts more and more each year.

Monsieur Chrono (Mr Stopwatch)

The Frenchman Jacques Anquetil gained his nickname on account of his time-trialling ability against the clock, but he needed a bit more than that to become the first man to win five Tours de France, and the first man to win all three Grand Tours. He achieved the Tour/Vuelta double in 1963 and the Tour/Giro double in 1964. He was never short of confidence, declaring before the 1961 Tour that he would take the yellow jersey on day one and wear it all the way to Paris – and he did. Like Fausto Coppi before him, he also provided the media with juicy scandals aplenty. He openly admitted taking drugs throughout his career, albeit at a time when it was pretty much de rigueur to do so and certainly before it became illegal; he partied well into the night between big stage races; and he gave the press a field day with some very colourful off-road relationships.

EDDY MERCKX

Born: Meensel, Belgium, 17 June 1945
Tour palmarès: General Classification 1969, 1970, 1971, 1972, 1974; Points Classification 1969, 1971, 1972; King of the Mountains 1969, 1970; Prix de la Combativité 1969, 1970, 1974, 1975; thirty-four stage wins
Nickname: the Cannibal

The modest Belgian Eddy Merckx is widely regarded to be the greatest rider of all time. He lived up to his nickname of 'the Cannibal' by gobbling up miles, trophies and records in a way that is unlikely ever to be surpassed. As far as the Tour is concerned, in addition to his record-equalling five Tour victories, he holds the records for most stage victories (thirty-four) and most days spent in the yellow jersey (ninety-six). He gave a taste of what was to come when he completed his first Tour in July 1969 (just hours before Neil Armstrong set foot on the moon), becoming the only man to simultaneously win all three of the main classifications and thereby have a choice of yellow, green and polka dot jerseys to wear as he celebrated his victories in Paris that evening.

During his illustrious career he also won five Giro d'Italia titles, three World Championships and one Vuelta a España. He is also one of only two riders (along with Stephen Roche of Ireland) to win cycling's Triple Crown by winning the Tour, the Giro and the World Championship in the same year (1974).

In 1996 the King of Belgium awarded him the ceremonial title of 'Baron', and in 2000 he was chosen as Belgium's 'Sports Figure of the Century'.

Le Blaireau (the Badger)

If anyone runs Eddy Merckx close as the greatest cyclist of all time, it is the man who took over his mantle as the sport's superstar – Bernard Hinault. Known as 'the Badger' because he was likened to the animal that never lets go of its prey, he dominated cycling in the late 1970s and early 1980s. Like Merckx before him, he could climb, sprint and time-trial. Like Merckx and Anquetil before him, he won the Tour de France five times, but he is the only man to finish in the top two of every Tour he completed. Having also won three Giri and two Vueltas, his ten Grand Tour victories are second only to the eleven won by Merckx, but he is the only man to have won all three Grand Tours more than once. He won twenty-eight individual Tour stages against Merckx's thirty-four. But whatever the record books might argue one way or the other, he was certainly no Eddie Merckx when it came to personality. He remains the last Frenchman to win the Tour de France (in 1985) but there are many who wish to this day that the accolade belonged to a rider with a bit more *je ne sais quoi*.

From Hero to Zero

The Texan Lance Armstrong was the most successful rider the Tour de France has ever seen, and now he isn't. Having recovered from life-threatening cancer, he won seven consecutive Tours from 1999 to 2005. In 2004 he became the first rider to win three consecutive mountain stages since the Italian Gino Bartali in 1948. Lauded by many, and by many Americans in particular, as an iconic superhero, he nonetheless rewrote the record books under a constant cloud of suspicion. There were continual hints and allegations that his sudden victory in 1999 and his domination of the Tour for the next seven years were too good to be true. A number of French journalists were particularly slow to cheer his victories and the cycling world remained split as Armstrong tested negative in hundreds of dope tests and openly ridiculed and even bullied his detractors. In 2012, all of the suspicions and accusations were proved to be true and Lance Armstrong fell to earth with a crash that was heard around the world. He was stripped of his titles and banned for life after a United States Anti-Doping Agency report stated that Armstrong, and the US Postal/Discovery Channel team he rode for, had enforced 'the most sophisticated, professionalized and successful doping program that sport has ever seen'. (See the chapter headed 'Doping and Cheating' for more information about this and the impact of doping generally within the sport of cycling.)

Big Mig

Following the removal of Lance Armstrong from the records, the Spaniard Miguel Indurain is the only man in history to win five consecutive Tours (1991–1995). His power came from unusual physiological traits: a big frame (for a cyclist), a lung capacity of almost 8 litres (the average man has 6) and a resting pulse of twenty-eight beats per minute (half the normal average), which meant his heart didn't have to work as hard and his blood could pump more oxygen around his body. Never all that popular with the French on account of his mechanical style, he was nonetheless voted Spain's 'Sportsman of the Century' ahead of Seve Ballesteros in 2000.

Allez la France! (Go France!)

Although their last victory was as long ago as 1985, France has provided by far the most Yellow Jersey winners in the history of the race, twenty-one cyclists providing thirty-six wins (five apiece having been supplied by Jacques Anquetil and Bernard Hinault). Belgium is in second place with ten riders providing eighteen wins (five of them courtesy of Eddy Merckx). Spain is in third place just ahead of Italy, thanks to two golden periods for Spanish riders, the first when Miguel Indurain won five consecutive Tours in the nineties and the second when three riders (Óscar Pereiro, Alberto Contador and Carlos Sastre) collectively secured four more consecutive wins between 2006 and 2009. (It would again have been five consecutive Spanish wins had Alberto Contador not been stripped of the 2010 title for doping.) When Australia (courtesy of Cadel Evans, the oldest post-war Tour winner at the grand old age of thirty-four) and the

United Kingdom (courtesy of Bradley Wiggins, sporting the longest post-war sideburns) added their names to the list in 2011 and 2012 respectively, the number of countries to have supplied Yellow Jersey winners rose to thirteen. Ireland's solitary win came courtesy of Stephen Roche in 1987, the year in which he joined Eddy Merckx as the only winner of cycling's 'triple crown' (winning the Tour, the Giro and the World Championship in the same year).

Yellow Jersey Winners by Nation

France	👕👕👕👕👕👕👕👕👕👕👕👕+	36
Belgium	👕👕👕👕👕👕👕👕👕👕+	18
Spain	👕👕👕👕👕👕👕👕👕👕👕+	12
Italy	👕👕👕👕👕👕👕👕👕	9
Luxembourg	👕👕👕👕👕	5
United States	👕👕👕	3
Netherlands	👕👕	2
Switzerland	👕👕	2
Denmark	👕	1
Germany	👕	1
Ireland	👕	1
Australia	👕	1
United Kingdom	👕	1

Top Guns

In 1953 the Swiss rider Fritz Schär was the first winner of what we know today as the Green Jersey competition, or Points Classification. From Germany Erik Zabel is the most successful sprinter in the history of the competition, with a record six (consecutive) wins between 1996 and 2001. Ireland's Sean Kelly comes next in the all-time standings, with four wins in the 1980s. Eddie Merckx is among five riders who won the competition three times. Only Eddie Merckx (three times) and Bernard Hinault have won the Green and Yellow Jersey competitions in the same Tour. The last French winner of the Green Jersey was Laurent Jalabert in 1995. Each generation produces its own Top Guns and more recent ones include our own Mark Cavendish and the talented Slovakian Peter Sagan.

Belgium has produced by far the greatest number of Green Jersey winners (nineteen), ahead of France (nine) and Germany (eight). This is primarily due to an astonishing period of eleven Belgian wins in thirteen years between 1969 and 1981, involving seven different riders and including three wins apiece for Eddy Merckx and Freddy Maertens.

Green Jersey Winners by Nation

Nation		Count
Belgium	👕👕👕👕👕👕👕👕👕👕+	19
France	👕👕👕👕👕👕👕👕👕	9
Germany	👕👕👕👕👕👕👕👕	8
Australia	👕👕👕👕	4
Ireland	👕👕👕👕	4
Netherlands	👕👕👕👕	4
Uzbekistan	👕👕👕	3
Italy	👕👕	2
Norway	👕👕	2
Switzerland	👕👕	2
Spain	👕	1
United Kingdom	👕	1
Slovakia	👕	1

SEAN KELLY

Born: Carrick-on-Suir, Ireland, 24 May 1956
Tour palmarès: Points Classification 1982,
1983, 1985, 1989; five stage wins
Nicknames: the New Cannibal, King Kelly

Farmer's son and former bricklayer Sean Kelly didn't just win four Green Jersey competitions at the Tour de France. He was one of the most successful riders of the 1980s and one of the great Classics winners of all time, including Paris-Nice seven years in a row. He was the first rider to be ranked number one when world rankings were introduced to cycling in 1984, a position he held on to for a record-breaking six years.

Although he is best remembered as a sprinter and Classics racer, he did in fact mature into a very good all-round bike rider. He was a formidable climber and an even more formidable descender. He could time-trial, and he was not afraid of instigating or going with breakaways. All of this resulted in him securing four top-ten Tour finishes, and in winning the Vuelta a España in 1988.

Nowadays, when he is not on his farm or riding for charity, he commentates on the Tour and other races for television, a remarkable progression for an Irish boy so taciturn that he was once prone to nodding his answers when asked questions during radio interviews.

The Manx Missile

The profile page on Mark Cavendish's website reads: **Fastest man on two wheels. FACT.**

It is a proud boast, but it is also one that he is entitled to make. The explosive bursts of speed that propel him to the finishing line had already resulted in twenty-three Tour de France stage wins by the end of the 2012 race – only Eddy Merckx, Bernard Hinault and André Leducq have won more, but nobody has won more in terms of mass-finish sprints alone. The world first took notice in 2008 when Cavendish took two stages in the Giro and four in the Tour at the age of just twenty-three. Records started to tumble as he blasted his way to six more Tour stage wins in 2009 alone. In 2011 he became the first-ever British winner of the Tour's Points Classification (Green Jersey), and within two months he had added a Rainbow Jersey by ending Britain's forty-six-year wait for a Road Race World Champion. He polished 2011 off with an MBE and an astonishing 49 per cent of the public vote to win the BBC Sports Personality of the Year trophy. In 2012 the 'Manx Missile' also became the first rider to win the final stage of the Tour on the Champs-Elysées in four consecutive years.

The Wakefield Missile

Less well known than the Manx Missile is the British sprinter whose records Cavendish has broken. Barry

Hoban won eight Tour stages between 1967 and 1975 (although he was allowed to win the first one in memory of Tom Simpson, who had collapsed and died the day before), a record he held until Cavendish soared past it in 2009. He was also the only British rider to win two consecutive Tour stages pre-Cavendish. He still holds the record for most Tours completed by a British rider (eleven), and one Hoban feat that Cavendish isn't likely to be repeating is that, most unusually for a specialist sprinter, Hoban also won a Tour mountain stage.

The Mountain Men

The Frenchman Richard Virenque tops the King of the Mountains table with seven wins between 1994 and 2004, including four consecutive wins from 1994 to 1997 (although his reputation was sullied as a central figure in the 1998 Festina affair – see the chapter headed 'Doping and Cheating' for more detail). Two riders have won six times: the Spaniard Federico Bahamontes between 1954 and 1964; and the Belgian Lucien van Impe between 1971 and 1983. Two all-time greats to have won the Polka Dot Jersey competition are Eddy Merckx (twice) and Bernard Hinault. The Frenchman Laurent Jalabert overcame recurring altitude sickness to win King of the Mountains in 2001 and 2002, thereby adding two polka dot jerseys to the two green ones he had won as a sprinter way back in 1992 and 1995 (he reinvented himself as an all-rounder after a sickening accident in 1994 put him off being involved in mass sprint finishes – see the 'Troubles and Tragedies' section in the chapter headed 'The Race' for more detail). The Belgian Félicien Vervaecke won the second of his polka dot jerseys in 1937 in spite of not finishing the Tour, something that would not be allowed nowadays. The winners in 2008 (Bernhard Kohl of Austria) and 2009 (Franco Pellizotti of Italy) have been expunged from the record books for doping offences.

The Glaswegian Vegetarian

Until Mark Cavendish joined him in 2011, the Glaswegian Robert Millar was the only Brit to have won a major Tour de France jersey, having won the King of the Mountains Classification in 1984. He remains the only English-speaking winner of the Polka Dot Jersey competition. He finished fourth overall in 1984, the highest finish for a British rider until Bradley Wiggins and Chris Froome surpassed him in 2012. He finished second overall in the Vueltas of 1985 and 1986, and won the Giro's King of the Mountains Classification in 1987, again finishing second overall.

Unusually for a bike racer, he partially attributed his successes to a strict vegetarian diet. It is often joked that you rarely hear 'Glaswegian' and 'vegetarian' in the same sentence, but it is even more unusual to hear 'Glaswegian', 'vegetarian' and 'Tour de France jersey winner' in the same sentence.

LUCIEN VAN IMPE

Born: Mere, Belgium, 20 October 1946
Tour palmarès: General Classification 1976; King of the Mountains 1971, 1972, 1975, 1977, 1981, 1983; nine stage wins
Nickname: de kleine van Mere (the Little Man from Mere)

Lucien van Impe was one of the great climbers, and a real Tour de France specialist. Not only did he win the GC in 1976 and King of the Mountains six times, he finished every single one of the fifteen Tours he started (only the Dutchman Joop Zoetemelk has finished more). He finished in the top three on five occasions and in the top ten in all but five of the fifteen Tours he started. He also won the King of the Mountains Classification twice in the Giro.

Locked in battle with Zoetemelk on the mountain climbs of stage 14 in the 1976 Tour, van Impe went so fast that forty-five of the ninety-three riders still in the race at the time ended the day outside the time limit and the organisers had to waive the elimination rule for that stage.

Van Impe's house in Mere is named 'Alpe d'Huez' in honour of the mountain where he first took the yellow jersey on the way to his one and only Tour win in 1976. When he came home that year, the bar where his supporters had gathered each day to follow him in the race was painted entirely yellow.

Peak Form

Of the seventy-one years in which the King of the Mountains Classification has been run since its inception in 1933, French riders have won a record twenty-one times, mainly due to a purple patch of ten wins in eleven years (1994–2004), a winning streak that was carelessly interrupted by the Colombian, Santiago Botero, in 2000. Next come the Spaniards (with seventeen wins), followed by the Italians (twelve). Robert Millar, as mentioned above, supplied the one British win in 1984.

Polka Dot Jersey Winners by Nation

France	👕👕👕👕👕👕👕👕👕👕+	21
Spain	👕👕👕👕👕👕👕👕👕👕+	17
Italy	👕👕👕👕👕👕👕👕👕👕👕+	12
Belgium	👕👕👕👕👕👕👕👕👕👕👕	11
Colombia	👕👕👕👕	4
Denmark	👕👕	2
Luxembourg	👕👕	2
Netherlands	👕👕	2
Switzerland	👕	1
United Kingdom	👕	1
Austria	👕	1

'It never gets easier; you just go faster.'

Greg LeMond, three-times Tour winner

The Clockwork Men

A time trial is often referred to as a 'race of truth', because there is no shelter or slipstream to be had from any other rider. You are on your own, and Tours can be won and lost on the times achieved against the clock – Jacques Anquetil built five Tour victories on solid time trials (see 'Monsieur Chrono' above). Of the 210 individual time trials run since they were introduced in 1934, fifty-six have been won by the four all-time greats of the Tour: Bernard Hinault tops the time-trial charts with nineteen, followed by Eddy Merckx (sixteen), Jacques Anquetil (eleven) and Miguel Indurain (ten). The Swiss rider Fabian Cancellara won his seventh time trial in 2012 and may yet add to his total. Lance Armstrong had eleven time-trial wins to his name, but now he has none.

Miles Ahead!

The engaging British rider Chris Boardman, now a popular TV presenter, won a total of three Tour prologue time trials during his career (Lille in 1994, Rouen in 1997 and Dublin in 1998). Because prologues always take place on day one of the Tour, these wins guaranteed that he got to wear the coveted yellow jersey in three separate years. Somewhat bizarrely, and quite appropriately given his propensity to eat them up, his middle name is Miles.

He recorded the fastest-ever time trial in 1994, when he completed a 7.2-km (4.5-mile) prologue course around Lille at an average speed of 55.152 kph (34.270 mph). He also posted the second-fastest average speed ever (54.193 kph/33.674 mph) in the 1997 prologue in Dublin. Fabian Cancellara came fairly close to the record in the London prologue of 2007 with an average speed of 53.660 kph (33.343 mph), but Boardman's record still stands.

Paris, Here I Come

The American Greg LeMond holds the record for the fastest average speed over a longer (i.e. non-prologue) time-trial course. He achieved 54.545 kph (33.893 mph) over 24.5 km (15.2 miles) in the final stage of the 1989 Tour, when he famously overcame a 50-second deficit between Versailles and Paris to beat the Frenchman Laurent Fignon by 8 seconds on the Champs-Elysées, thereby achieving the second of his three Tour wins. This remains the smallest winning margin in the Tour's history. LeMond's average speed that day was slightly slower than the record speed that Boardman had achieved five years earlier, but it is arguably way more impressive when you consider the much longer distance he travelled over and the fact that he did it on race day 21, after crossing the Pyrenees and the Alps, whereas Boardman achieved his record on day one, while relatively fresh as a daisy.

A Real Turkey Shoot!

In 1987, while back in America recovering from a racing accident, Greg LeMond went on a turkey shoot in the foothills of the Sierra Nevada with his uncle and brother-in-law. Upon hearing movement behind him, the brother-in-law turned and fired through a bush, hitting LeMond in the back and side with sixty pellets. His injuries were near fatal and he had lost 65 per cent of his blood by the time he received emergency surgery to repair his right lung. It was 1989 before he could return to the Tour and he must have been a bit nervous waiting for the starter pistol that year.

Time After Time

Of the 210 time trials competed for in the Tour's history, France has produced by far the greatest number of wins (fifty-nine). Over half of those French wins came from Anquetil and Hinault alone. Next comes Belgium (thirty-eight), then Spain (twenty-two). Great Britain has enjoyed eight time-trial victories, courtesy of Chris Boardman, Bradley Wiggins, David Millar and Sean Yates. The USA has won three time trials courtesy of Greg LeMond and won and lost eleven courtesy of Lance Armstrong.

SIR BRADLEY WIGGINS

Born: Ghent, Belgium, 28 April 1980
Tour palmarès: General Classification 2012 (including two stage wins)
Nickname: Wiggo

David Hasselhoff has a rival for the title of 'Knight Rider'. It is Sir Bradley Wiggins, knight of the road; the first British rider to win the Tour de France; the first man in history to do so in the same year as winning an Olympic gold medal; one of the few men in history to achieve major success on the track and on the road (he has seven Olympic medals in all, four of them gold). He was the BBC Sports Personality of the Year 2012 and was knighted by Her Majesty the Queen in the 2013 New Year's Honours List.

His earlier training and experience on the track had proved to be a solid base for success as a time triallist but he needed to retrain and slim down if he was going to be good enough as an all-rounder capable of winning the Tour. Under the wing of Dave Brailsford and the Sky Procycling team, he did just that. Fast enough to win two individual time trials in the 2012 Tour, and slim and fit enough to climb in the mountains, the historic achievement of being the first British rider to wear yellow on the Champs-Elysées podium was his.

'Wiggo' also knows how to work a crowd, whether playing guitar on stage with fellow 'mod' Paul Weller, or being interviewed, in French, by French television – the French love a non-French rider who takes the trouble to speak their language. *Vive le Wiggo!*

Time Trial Wins by Nation

Nation	Wins
France	59
Belgium	38
Spain	22
Switzerland	16
Netherlands	14
Germany	11
Italy	10
United Kingdom	8
Luxembourg	5
United States	3
Australia	3

The Young Ones

In the thirty-eight years since the Young Rider Classification (now also known as the White Jersey competition) was introduced in 1975 for riders under the age of twenty-six, two riders have won it three times: Jan Ullrich of Germany (1996–1998) and Andy Schleck of Luxembourg (2008–2010). The Italian Marco Pantani is the only other rider to win the award more than once (in 1994 and 1995).

Clean Sweep

If the Young Rider Classification had existed in 1969, Eddy Merckx would have won a white jersey to go with the yellow, green and polka dot jerseys that he did actually win that year.

Most Aggressive Riders

In the sixty years that that the Prix de la Combativité has been awarded to the most attacking rider over the whole Tour, Eddy Merckx (surprise, surprise!) has won it the most times (four), ahead of Bernard Hinault (three) and Richard Virenque (three). Tellingly, Eddy Merckx won the award in both of the years that followed the last of his five Yellow Jersey victories, so he was still trying! Bernard Hinault, in 1981, was the last rider to be crowned the super-combatif in the same year as winning the Yellow Jersey competition. Recent winners include the Frenchman Jérémy Roy (2011) and the Dane Chris Anker Sørenson (2012).

To say that French riders try hard in the Tour de France would be something of an understatement. Of the sixty Prix de la Combativité awards since 1953, twenty-nine wins have been by French riders. There is then something of a chasm to Belgium (six), Spain (six) and Netherlands (five). Only five other countries have supplied a winner. Since a Frenchman last won the Yellow Jersey in 1985, over 50 per cent of super-combatifs have been French. Mock their lack of recent GC success if you will, but never accuse them of not trying!

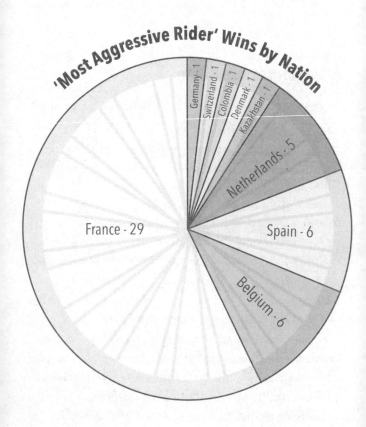

'Most Aggressive Rider' Wins by Nation

Germany - 1
Switzerland - 1
Colombia - 1
Denmark - 1
Kazakhstan - 1
Netherlands - 5
Spain - 6
Belgium - 6
France - 29

One Day at a Time

Never think for a moment that it doesn't matter that much
to win a single stage in a Tour. It matters hugely, especially
if you only win one solitary stage in your whole career.
Like the teenage Italian Fabio Battesini, the youngest-ever
Tour de France stage winner, aged just nineteen when
he won the third stage of the 1931 Tour. It was to be his
first and his last stage victory, but nobody could ever
take it away from him. Winning any stage is like scoring
the winning goal in a cup final. It secures immediate
fame, especially if you're French, in which case you are
immediately elevated to the status of national hero.
Although it is possible to win the Tour without winning a
single stage along the way (this has happened six times),
it is probably much less fun for the rider concerned, and
it is most definitely much less fun for the spectators, who
are thereby deprived of the sight of the conquering hero
crossing the line ahead of the other rider-warriors, arms
aloft at the moment of triumph.

But for some, stage wins become positively habit-
forming. Thirty-one riders have won ten or more stages
of the Tour. Eddy Merckx has won the most (thirty-four),
followed by Bernard Hinault (twenty-eight) and André
Leducq (twenty-five). Mark Cavendish is gaining on them
fast, with twenty-three wins already under his saddle.
Cavendish has the most mass-finish stage wins in the
history of the race, all twenty-three of his stage wins (up
to 2012) being sprint finishes, ahead of André Darrigade

and André Leducq (with twenty-two), François Faber (nineteen) and Eddy Merckx (eighteen). Three riders have won eight stages in a single Tour: Charles Pélissier (France) in 1930, Eddy Merckx in 1970 and 1974, and Merckx's fellow Belgian Freddy Maertens in 1976.

Tour Stage Winners by Nation

France	690
Belgium	467
Italy	257
Netherlands	167
Spain	123
Luxembourg	70
Germany	61
Switzerland	60
United Kingdom	51
Australia	23
United States	20

Riders from thirty-two countries have won at least one stage of the Tour. France is way out in front with 690 stage wins, followed by Belgium with 467 and Italy with 257. The United Kingdom lies in ninth place (with fifty-one wins), primarily thanks to the stage wins supplied in recent years by Mark Cavendish. Brazil, Canada, Poland, South Africa and Sweden have each provided a solitary stage winner.

L'année des Rosbifs
(The Year of the Brits)

The year 2012 provided a vintage Tour for *les rosbifs* (as the French endearingly refer to the Brits). Not only did British riders take first (Bradley Wiggins) AND second place (Chris Froome) in the GC, they also won seven out of the twenty-one stages of the race (three sprint-finish wins for Cavendish, two time-trial wins for Wiggins and a stage win each for Chris Froome and David Millar). But there was some joy for the French hosts as their popular countryman Thomas Voeckler won the King of the Mountains Classification that year, so the Brits didn't quite have the whole roast beef to themselves.

Chapter 3

Team Spirit

'We are always striving for improvement,
for those one per cent gains, in
absolutely every single thing we do.'

**Dave Brailsford, referring to the philosophy
that has brought success to the British
Olympic and Sky Procycling teams**

The well-organised, well-drilled teams that we see
today were simply not welcome in the early years of the
Tour. In fact, Henri Desgrange would impose severe
penalties on a rider found to be accepting help of any
kind, or found to be in collusion with any other rider.
Teamwork simply went against his idea that the race
should be about individual strength and endurance.
And the idea of trade-sponsored teams was anathema
to him, because he feared the influence over the race
they would demand in return.

The Youth of '67

In reverting to national teams for the 1967 Tour, the organisers tried to spice things up a bit by allowing countries to enter youth teams in addition to their A teams. France entered two such teams: Les Bleuets (the Little Blues) and Les Coqs (the Cockerels). Belgium entered the Red Devils, Spain entered team Esperanza (Hope) and Italy entered team Primavera (Springtime). The youngsters of Les Bleuets and Primavera both held the overall race lead at one point, and team Primavera finished a very creditable third, not far behind 'Big France' and 'Big Netherlands'. A fully grown British team finished last.

In 1930 Desgrange finally accepted that teams might add an interesting extra dimension to the Tour but, still set against team sponsorship, he insisted that only national teams could compete. France won the first-ever Team Classification that year and went on to win nine of the twenty-five national team races that occurred until 1961, when trade-sponsored teams heralded the modern way of funding major sporting events. Belgium went one better with ten wins over that period, including a win for the Belgium B Team in 1939 (France and Belgium had been invited to enter additional teams because Germany, Italy and Spain were more preoccupied with matters of war than of sport at the time). The organisers did revert temporarily to national teams in 1967 (won by France, thereby equalling the ten wins of Belgium) and 1968 (won by Spain, which remains the last country to have won a Tour de France Team Classification).

Team Wins by Nation

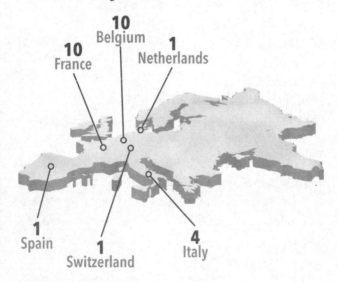

10
Belgium

1
Netherlands

10
France

1
Spain

1
Switzerland

4
Italy

Trade-sponsored Teams

The first official trade-sponsored teams competed in the Tour in 1962, but they still had to have a national flavour to them, so the fifteen teams of ten riders had to have at least six riders of the same nationality. The winning team, sponsored by ACCB-Saint Raphael-Helyett-Hutchinson, a bike-manufacturing conglomerate, had French riders as its required majority and included the great Jacques Anquetil on his way to becoming the first five-times winner of the Yellow Jersey. The same team, but not all the same riders, won the following year, but not before being renamed Saint Raphael-Géminiani-Dunlop, thereby setting a trend of confusion that has been with us ever since.

Sponsors over the years have included a number of bike manufacturers, as well as manufacturers of cars, mobile phones, beer, soft drinks, disposable pens and razors, electronics, chemicals, watches, jeans, sportswear, espresso machines and satnavs, not to mention supermarkets, health food providers, banks, Internet service providers, TV stations, a Spanish lottery for the blind, the US Postal Service and a coalition of Kazakh state-owned companies.

Many sponsors must have been delighted with increased sales over the years; others may have rued the day they ever got involved when riders of the teams they supported got kicked out/banned/arrested/publicly humiliated for doping offences. Although, perhaps on the basis that no publicity is bad publicity, the US Postal Service is still very likely to be selling stamps by the million.

Hold that Name!

It is not easy to tell which 'trade teams'
dominated which periods in the race's history,
because not many of them have held on to their
names, never mind their riders, long enough to
dominate anything for any length of time. By
way of example, a T-Mobile team did manage
to win three consecutive Tours between 2003
and 2005, having enjoyed success previously
as the German-based Team Telekom, and
eventually morphing into the American-based
HTC-Highroad via incarnations as Team High
Road, Team Columbia, Team Columbia-High
Road, Team Columbia-HTC, and Team HTC-
Columbia. The team folded in 2011 after a lot
of very successful years under the American
Bob Stapleton, and hard on the heels of the
Tour de France in which Mark Cavendish
won the Green Jersey competition for them.

Here are some more examples of
longstanding 'teams' that were not always
visible as such to the naked eye:

Gitane/Renault-Elf/Castorama: A talent-spotting, Tour-winning machine under the direction of Cyrille Guimard for thirty years from the 1960s onwards. Won the Tour with Lucien van Impe, Bernard Hinault, Greg LeMond and Laurent Fignon.

Peugeot/Z/Gan/Crédit Agricole: Under Roger Legeay the personnel and team structure remained largely the same for forty years from the 1960s onwards. Riders included Eddy Merckx, Tom Simpson, Bernard Thévenet, Robert Millar, Stephen Roche, Greg LeMond, Thor Hushovd and Chris Boardman.

Reynolds/Banesto/Baleares/Caisse d'Epargne: Longstanding Spanish team under José Miguel Echávarri since the 1980s. Won seven Tours with Miguel Indurain, Pedro Delgado and Óscar Pereiro. Echávarri retired in 2008 and the team has since morphed into Movistar.

US Postal/Discovery Channel: The team remained together throughout the Lance Armstrong years but never won the Team Classification as all their efforts were geared towards securing Armstrong's seven (illicit) Yellow Jersey wins.

Hold that Rider!

It can be just as difficult for teams to hold on to riders as it is to hold on to names. Although riders, as in any sport, might move on to earn more money, or because they are uncomfortable for whatever reason within a particular team environment, sometimes it is just a case of good, old-fashioned career progression. Take Mark Cavendish. He served his apprenticeship in 2005–2006 with Team Sparkasse, a feeder team for T-Mobile. After showing some promise, he was promoted to T-Mobile, where he enjoyed unprecedented success until the team disbanded (as HTC-Highroad) in 2011. He joined Team Sky in 2012 to be a part of the British success story that year but, on realising that even Team Sky could not support simultaneous bids for the GC and Green Jersey competitions, he left to continue his quest for sprinting immortality with Omega Pharma – Quick-Step.

Team Strategy, Composition and Tactics

In accordance with UCI (Union Cycliste Internationale) rules, the (currently eighteen) UCI Pro Teams are automatically entered to compete in the Tour, with the organisers retaining the right to select additional teams from the UCI Professional Continental Tour. Four such teams were added in 2012, bringing the total number of nine-man teams to twenty-two.

The composition of each team is determined by the strategic aims of sponsors and management. Unless the top rider has all the qualities of Eddy Merckx (in which case, just give him free rein to do whatever he likes and ask the other eight to do their best to keep up while he clean-sweeps the jerseys), the team will try to build the team around him, thereby increasing their chances of winning one of the major classifications. The Team Classification is generally considered less important than the main individual classifications and a team would not normally enter the Tour with the primary aim of winning the team prize.

Team Sky's main rider in 2012 was Bradley Wiggins and their strategic objective was to secure the General Classification for a British rider for the first time in history. It was the role of the other team members to protect him at all times, for example by shielding him during certain stages from other riders or from headwinds or crosswinds, and to ensure that he was fed and watered the right amounts at the right times.

HTC-Highroad's star in 2011 was Mark Cavendish and, in addition to offering him protection in the ways described above for Bradley Wiggins, he also needed riders who had the ability and experience to deliver him to the front of the lead-out train at the right time to win enough sprint stages to secure victory in the Points Classification.

Un 'Bon Rouleur'

The *rouleurs* of any team are the riders
who set the pace, who offer protection
against the elements, who break themselves
for the greater good of the team. They
rarely get individual glory. They always
get a lot of respect. If you hear a French
TV commentator referring to you as
'un bon rouleur', be very flattered. They
mean it as a huge compliment.

If a team's main aim is to win the King of the Mountains
Classification, it needs to enlist as many strong climbers
as it can get its hands on, and no sprinters. And so on.
But whatever the overall strategy, the team needs to be
a team. Ideally, a team needs a maximum of one prima
donna and at least two or three *rouleurs* to do the really
hard work.

Tactics will vary from day to day, depending on
the type of stage involved, the terrain, the weather
conditions, and the health and fitness of the team
members. The *directeur sportif* (team director) will
direct the day-to-day strategy and hour-to-hour tactics
on the road from the lead support car, using two-way
radio to instruct his riders and to receive feedback
from those riders on what is happening up ahead.

Team cars also carry any supplies that might be needed by their riders during the course of the race, including water bottles, nutrition bars, extra clothing, spare wheels and, of course, the ubiquitous bikes on the roof. They can offer mechanical help (a mechanic will always ride in the team car) and first aid during the race. A back-up support car will also be on hand in the follow-up convoy of team cars that must remain at least two hundred metres behind the main convoy. (This is all a far cry from the early motor cars that often struggled in the early years of the race to keep the teams' 'suited and booted' management up with the bikes on steep climbs.)

If they're out to try and win a sprint stage, a team will need to try and dictate the pace of the race, and keep itself together so that it can change pacemakers at the most appropriate times. That same team on a mountain stage might spend the day protecting and encouraging each other on the slopes, in order to ensure that the whole team finishes within the time limit for the stage, having expended the least amount of energy in the process.

If a team is not likely to be competing for the major prizes in the first place, the tactics might be to allow one or more riders to go for glory within breakaway groups on one or more individual stages. Even if it doesn't pay off in a surprise stage win, the team's sponsors will love the airplay and the riders will gain valuable experience.

The Brailsford Touch

Sir Dave Brailsford is a British sporting phenomenon. Having secured unprecedented success as the manager of the British cycling team at the Beijing Olympics in 2008, primarily with track cycling, he decided to see if he could employ the same nth-degree planning and execution to similar effect in Continental-style road racing. He could, and he did. Along with his right-hand man, the Australian Shane Sutton, he set up Team Sky from scratch in 2009 and within three years he had delivered the first British winner in the history of the Tour de France. His philosophy is that small, incremental improvements to everything – bikes, skinsuits, nutrition, altitude training, etc., etc., etc. – result in sufficient overall gain to make a real difference. He's not wrong, apparently. Further success at the 2012 London Olympics and Paralympics resulted in Her Majesty adding a knighthood to the MBE and CBE she had already bestowed on him in previous years.

Nine-a-side?

It does, in fact, take rather more than nine bike riders to compete as a team in the Tour de France. Once you add in mechanics, trainers, doctors, physios, chiropractors, masseurs, chefs, nutritionists (riders can burn up to nine thousand calories and lose up to two kilos in a single stage, so chef and nutritionist are very important jobs!), managers, technicians, *soigneurs* (the guys who make sure that everybody else gets to and from races and hotels, and ensure that race clothing and food and drink packs are in the right place at the right time, and a lot more besides), drivers, transporters, enough PR people to ensure value for money for sponsors and feed the social media, the overall number of people on the team is, well, more than nine.

How to Grow Your Business Overnight

Incroyable! US firm Motorola reckoned that public knowledge of their mobile phone brand went almost overnight from zero to 75 per cent across Europe after they took over sponsorship of the previously named 7-Eleven team in time for the 1990 Tour de France. Motorola went on to introduce the two-way radio system that is now in common use between riders and their team managers.

Chapter 4

Racing Machines

'The cyclist is a man half made of flesh and half of steel, that only our century of science and iron could have spawned.'

**Louis Baudry de Saunier,
nineteenth-century French writer**

A lot of people have been taking the production of road-racing bicycles very seriously for a very long time. From the classic steel frames of the pioneering early manufacturers like Peugeot to the twentieth-first-century nanotechnology experts who search for marginal gains in every aerodynamic nook and mechanical cranny, the pursuit of ultimate harmony between man and bike goes on.

In 1903 Maurice Garin rode a Française bike to victory. In 2012 Bradley Wiggins won the race on a Pinarello. The two bikes were remarkably similar, in the sense that they both had a frame, two wheels and a saddle. Looked at a little more closely, though, there were in fact some considerable differences. For example, Garin's steel bike weighed 18 kg (40 lbs) and had one fixed gear. Wiggins's carbon-fibre bike weighed less than 7 kg (15 lbs) and had twenty gears.

Altogether Now!

In 1930, in yet another attempt to keep bike manufacturers firmly in their place, Henri Desgrange forced all riders to use the same yellow, steel bike that he himself supplied. The organisers continued to supply standard bikes to competitors until the outbreak of World War Two, denying bike manufacturers the publicity they so desperately sought to increase their sales.

Raw Materials

Steel

There was probably something inherently appropriate about the original men of steel riding bikes of steel on pedal power alone, and steel wasn't to disappear any time soon either. The most effective steel tubing from the late 1950s until the early 1990s was the British-made Reynolds 531, and Miguel Indurain was the last rider to win a Tour on a steel-framed bike, in 1994.

Alloy

Luis Ocaña (1973) and Greg LeMond (1991) won on titanium bikes, and the 1990s also saw wins on combined aluminium and ceramic (Miguel Indurain in 1995 and Bjarne Riis in 1996) and on aluminium alone (Jan Ullrich in 1997 and Marco Pantani in 1998).

Carbon Fibre

This material first saw victory with Lance Armstrong in 1999, and has seen nothing but victory since. This extra-strong yet super-light polymer soon spread from the frame to other parts of the bike – rims, spokes, seat posts, cranks, stems and handlebars. And it has become ever stronger and ever lighter, to the extent that the Tour's organisers now insist on a minimum weight (6.8 kg/15 lbs) for the bikes used in the race in order to ensure that the Tour remains a relatively even contest (all other things being equal) on similarly specified machines.

British Steel

The Reynolds Tube Co. Ltd of Birmingham supplied the steel-tubed frames for the bicycles that were ridden to almost thirty Tour victories between 1958 (Charly Gaul) and 1991 (Miguel Indurain). Jacques Anquetil, Bernard Hinault and Laurent Fignon all also won the Tour on Reynolds-framed bikes.

Reynolds have been making steel tubes for well over a century, and a Reynolds-tubed bike can be found just about anywhere on the planet. Bike-frame tubing was either too weak or too heavy until Alfred Reynolds worked out in 1897 how to 'butt' tubes of different thicknesses together. They employ the same mechanical principles today, using the same secret 'recipe', but working with sheet metal manufactured to aerospace standards. If you need to re-enter the earth's atmosphere on a bike, make sure it's a bike made with Reynolds tubing.

Drawing Boards and Laboratories

Design improvements have run in parallel with changes to the raw materials used. Once the organisers' shackles were finally removed and bikes had modern equipment like gears and non-wooden wheel rims, the designers could get drawing on their drawing boards and the technicians could get labbing in their labs (and, more recently, in their wind tunnels). Frames got smaller, wheelbases got shorter, tubes got slopier, tyres got narrower, pedals got clipless, gears got batteries, and straight lines got curves.

More recent advances include electronic groupsets (more of which later) and a wider range of gearing choices – legendary climbers of the past like Lucien Van Impe had to ride out of the saddle pushing high gears for hours at a time; climbers today are better able to match their gearing to the challenge and climb at a more reasonable cadence. But bikes didn't just become more aerodynamic and efficient as a result of all this science, they became sexier as well.

The Glamorous Supermodels

So let's leave the science behind for a while and get excited about some of the supermodels of the sport. Let us admire the classic elegance of some early European models, wax lyrical about some enduring British national treasures, and gasp at the futuristic appeal of some American newcomers.

Peugeot

The lion of Peugeot roared early in the Tour de France, being ridden to victory in four consecutive years between 1905 and 1908, and in 1907 the first five bikes home were all Peugeots. Appropriately enough for a French manufacturer, it went on to amass a record-breaking total of ten Tour victories by 1977, when their countryman Bernard Thévenet secured their final victory. Thévenet (1975 and 1977) and Lucien Petit-Breton (1907 and 1908) had secured two French victories apiece on board Peugeot bikes. The Belgian Philippe Thys had also won twice on Peugeots just before the outbreak of World War One.

Pinarello

Pinarello racing models have been ridden to nine Tour victories in just over twenty years, including Miguel Indurain's victories in the early 1990s. Bradley Wiggins secured the ninth brand success in 2012 on the asymmetrically designed Pinarello Dogma2 (asymmetrical design allows better balance because it recognises that a bike cannot possibly be the same weight on both sides, as most of the mechanics, e.g. the chain, are to one side only).

Pinarello also have a long legacy of providing state-of-the-art time-trial bikes – the one they provided for Indurain in the 1990s was impressively aerodynamic for its time and Wiggins won the time trial that secured the Yellow Jersey in 2012 on the Pinarello Graal time-trial model.

The ladies have not been left out when it comes to Tour success on a Pinarello. The Lithuanian Edita Pučinskaitė rode one to victory in the 1998 Tour Féminin (see chapter headed 'The Race' for more information about the Tour Féminin).

Black Beginnings

Giovanni 'Nane' Pinarello had such little success as a pro racer that he suffered the ignominy in 1951 of wearing the *maglia nera*, the black jersey that was worn at the time by the rider at the back of the Giro d'Italia. The following year his team offered him 100,000 lire to give up his place to another rider. He took the money and started his own bike business. He was to prove a little bit better at making bikes than racing them.

Bianchi

Some bikes become synonymous with their riders, and none more so than the Bianchi with Fausto Coppi. On the way to winning his second Tour in 1952, the legendary Italian climber attacked on his celeste green Bianchi with still 6 km (3.7 miles) to go to the ski station at the top of l'Alpe d'Huez. It was decisive and it was captured for the first time by live television cameras. The legend of Fausto Coppi and his striking 1952 Bianchi was sealed forever, although arguments continue to this day over whether the distinctive colour of Bianchi bikes is in fact more 'duck egg blue' than 'celeste green'. At the speed Coppi climbed mountains, it was almost certainly impossible to tell as he sped past.

Coppi's other win in 1949 had also been on a Bianchi and another Italian climber, Marco Pantani, would add a third victory for the brand in 1998.

Merckx

Eddy Merckx largely rode his own-brand bikes to victory when he was rewriting the record books in the 1960s and 1970s. Although the frames were actually built by Italian stalwarts such as Faliero Masi and Ugo De Rosa (Merckx being a bit too busy at the time to build them himself), he himself remained an obsessive driving force behind the technical design and manufacturing process. He would demand up to fifty bikes a year and travel with more bikes than he could possibly need for most races.

In order to fill the void he felt following retirement from professional racing, Merckx then set about building his own bikes for the next generation. In this way, his name had returned to the peloton by 1982 and it has rarely been absent since.

Raleigh

This Nottingham-based company with the heron logo has been a world market leader since the nineteenth century, but it has enjoyed little racing success because it always sought primarily to produce family-oriented bikes – fun for the children, and reliable and affordable for the grown-ups. In 1980, though, Raleigh did provide the one and only British bike to win the Tour de France, ridden by the Dutchman Joop Zoetemelk for the Dutch TI-Raleigh Creda team (it was Zoetemelk's only Tour victory but he did complete the Tour a record-breaking sixteen times and finish runner-up a record-breaking six times).

Raleigh did come ridiculously close to enjoying a second Tour win in 1989 when the firm favourite, yellow-jersey-wearing Frenchman Laurent Fignon, lined up for the final day's time trial in Paris. He was a massive 50 seconds ahead of American Greg LeMond, he only had 24.5 km (15.2 miles) to travel and he was on a Raleigh! LeMond was riding a Bottecchia, a bike that had enabled fewer Tour victories than Raleigh had (i.e. none). What could possibly go wrong? (Answer: an unprecedented 58-second swing in favour of the American that had them crying in the streets of Nottingham.)

Scott

Having started off making ski equipment, the US firm founded by Ed Scott went on to change the shape of bicycle handlebars in a way that enabled the 'skier's tuck' position to be adopted during time trials. This was put to good use in the final time-trial stage of the 1989 Tour when American rider Greg LeMond upset all the odds to pip Laurent Fignon for the Yellow Jersey.

Twenty years later, Scott supplied Britain's Mark Cavendish with the featherweight carbon-fibre Scott Addict frame that Cavendish rode to his famous six stage wins in the 2009 Tour.

Bomber Control

The bombers of World War Two inspired the eye-catching decals (customised graphics) of the metallic grey frame of Cavendish's 2009 Scott Addict. These included a glamorous pin-up girl and space to mark the six 'kills' chalked up by the Manx Missile during the course of the race.

Trek

This US giant, founded by Dick Burke in 1976 in Wisconsin, was an early adopter and first-class developer of lightweight carbon-fibre frames. Trek went on to supply Lance Armstrong with one iconic bike after another, including the Madone 5.9 road frame and the Futuroscope TT and TTX time-trial bikes. There is little doubt that Armstrong's Tour

LE TOUR DE FRANCE

victories rocketed the Trek name into the stratosphere and the company is probably more entitled than any other to have mixed feelings about its long association with the fallen hero.

Shut Up Legs!

The evergreen, and ever-popular, German rider Jens Voigt has an impressive decal on the top tube of his Trek Madone 7 bike. In addition to his catchphrase 'Shut Up Legs' (he once famously said that this was what his brain told his legs when they started to hurt), it lists the impressive stats he has built up during his longstanding career as a professional racer, including the twenty-five screws that hold his broken bones together:

> **SHUT UP LEGS!**
> **805000 KM**
> **3100 KG OF PASTA CONSUMED**
> **110 STITCHES**
> **100 CRASHES**
> **64 WINS**
> **40 YEARS**
> **25 SCREWS**
> **16 TIMES AROUND THE WORLD**
> **11 BROKEN BONES**
> **1 JENS!**

Le Vélo aux Papillons
(the Butterfly Bike)

Even controversial British artist Damien Hirst got involved in iconic bike design, personalising the Trek Madone that Lance Armstrong rode into Paris at the end of the 2007 Tour. In typical Hirst fashion, his design drew interest and criticism in equal measure – interest because he covered the frame and wheels with butterfly images, criticism from animal rights activists because he used real butterflies!

The Fast Show

Time-trial bicycles might have the looks to turn heads, but that's not their point. Their point is they are fast, faster even than 'ordinary' professional road-racing bikes. When hundredths of a second count, only the lightest weights, fastest gear shifts and most aerodynamic bicycles will do. Some recent high-tech models not yet mentioned in this chapter include the following merchants of speed:

- **Ag2R La Mondiale Kuota Kalibur:** designed with ultra-compact seat and handlebars, with the handlebars positioned well below the seat to ensure the best aerodynamic profile for the rider, and with tubular wheels that are thinner on the inside near the spokes to reduce weight to an absolute minimum.

- **Cervélo P5:** its aerodynamic frame is claimed to take 30 seconds off a 40-kilometre time trial. Even the cables going to the gearbox are hidden inside a bar to avoid drag. Other features include integrated hydraulic brakes and a system embedded within the front aerobar (handlebars) for delivery of fluids and nutrition to the rider throughout the race.

- **BMC TimeMachine TM01:** Nanolight technology, with battery-powered electronic components inside the frame to help the bike adjust aerodynamically throughout the run.

- **Cannondale Slice RS:** perhaps the most magnificently named bike of all, especially once you realise that the RS stands for 'rocket ship'! Who wouldn't want a Cannondale Slice Rocket Ship? Everything is ultra-skinny, right down to the almost invisible seat post, and there isn't even a steer tube to pick up drag.

Tours Won by Bicycle Manufacturer

French manufacturers are way out in front when it comes to overall Tour victories, owing to the huge start they had after bagging the first twenty available. Peugeot, Gitane and Alycon have all contributed significantly to French dominance. Italian manufacturers come next, primarily on account of the Pinarello years of Miguel Indurain. The Americans are moving up the ranks, always assuming that their Trek wins are not struck from the records on account of 'the Armstrong effect'.

Tour Victories by Bicycle Manufacturer

Peugeot (FRA)	○○○○○○○○○○	10
Gitane (FRA)	○○○○○○○○○	9
Pinarello (ITA)	○○○○○○○○○	9
Trek (USA)	○○○○○○○○○	9
Alycon (FRA)	○○○○○○○	7
Automoto (FRA)	○○○○	4
Merckx (BEL)	○○○○	4
Bianchi (ITA)	○○○	3
Helyett (FRA)	○○○	3

Incroyable!

Now Where Did I Put that Spanner?

Groupsets were first used in the 1937 Tour, the winning components being supplied by the French company Super Champion. The only way a Tour rider had been allowed to 'change gears' before 1937 was to dismount and remove and turn his rear wheel in order to change it from uphill to downhill mode or vice versa.

The Not-quite-so-glamorous Groupsets

Although the supermodel bike frame gets most of the attention and glory, nowadays it's not going to start, speed up, slow down or stop without a groupset, which integrates the drivetrain (chains, cranksets, cassettes and levers) and braking components.

The Italian groupset manufacturer Campagnolo has 'won' forty of the seventy Tours since groupsets were first allowed in 1937, and pretty much dominated from the sixties through to the end of the nineties, including providing the components for all of the Tour victories of Bernard Hinault, Eddy Merckx and Miguel Indurain.

Shimano finally kicked Campagnolo off the top groupset spot in 1999 and have not looked back since. They provided the winning groupsets all through the Lance Armstrong years and for the Tour victories of Cadel Evans in 2011 and Bradley Wiggins in 2012, both of whom used the state-of-the-art Shimano Di2 electronic groupset (an electronic groupset allows for faster changing of gears through electronic switches that are connected to a small electric motor that moves the chain from cog to cog).

SRAM has joined these two giants on the 'groupset podium' since their components took Alberto Contador to actual Tour victory in 2009 and to disqualified Tour victory in 2010 (but, as luck would have it, the recorded winner, Andy Schleck, also happened to be using SRAM components).

All this sophisticated electronic 'road componentry' may one day become commonplace and thereby consign bicycle cables to the dustbin of history. Until then, even if you are unlikely to find yourself in front of the television shouting 'Come on, the rider with the SRAM Red, Black Edition, groupset', feel free to be impressed by the racing technology anyway.

Wheels and Tyres

But let us not forget the only two parts of the man and machine combination that actually touch the surface of the earth during a race. The two large round bits of the bike.

In the early days of the Tour all bikes had wooden wheels and riders carried spare tubular rubber tyres across their shoulders so that they could carry out their own puncture repairs as the race progressed. Although aluminium wheels were available by 1926, they were not allowed in the Tour until 1931. Nowadays carbon fibre is the common raw material of racing wheels. Other design and technological improvements to individual wheel components like the spokes have brought us to the reliable, ultra-light, super-efficient wheels of today. And spokes have even been dispensed with entirely in the solid disc wheels used by some riders to improve aerodynamics during time trials.

It's not always easy to tell which manufacturer's wheels which riders are using, either because they source different component parts, like rims and hubs, from different manufacturers (notwithstanding general sponsorship responsibilities), or because they want to keep some secret or other from their rivals. But we do know that the big names to provide wheels to successful Tour riders include Mavic, Shimano, ZIPP, Bontrager, Campagnolo and Reynolds, and that it does no harm to their general sales levels to point out their Tour successes to the world. By way of example, Mavic provided the winning wheels for seven out of twenty-one stages in the 2011 Tour, courtesy of the Garmin-Cervélo and Omega Pharma-Lotto teams, followed by five stage wins apiece for Shimano, involving four different teams, and ZIPP, all five wins coming courtesy of Mark Cavendish riding for HTC-Highroad. Advertising doesn't get much better than the Manx Missile riding your wheels to victory on the Champs-Elysées.

As for tyres, they remain largely 'tubular' to this day, but have never been without their problems. Even in the twenty-first century whole bikes have had to be changed mid-race when the glue that attaches tubular tyres to their wheel rims has melted in the heat.

An ongoing issue for racers is whether to use 'tubulars' or 'clinchers', clinchers being woven-fabric (e.g. nylon) tyres that are 'clinched' together with beading. Tubulars are still widely favoured in racing circles for a number of reasons: they're safer in the event of a puncture; they generally offer better cornering; they're usually lighter as part of a wheel-tyre system; and they're more supple and thus deliver a better feel for the road.

However, clinchers are said to travel faster than tubulars, and this is of particular interest to time-trial specialists, because the claimed extra safety, durability and comfort margins of tubulars are not such big issues over the course of a short time trial. The manufacturer Specialized has been capitalising on that fact with a special new time-trial-specific clincher, developed with the Omega Pharma – Quick-Step team and used by Tony Martin in the 2012 Tour. But clinchers are not exactly new to the Tour. In the 1980s Miguel Indurain was using them for downhill descents, as tubulars tended to overheat under his weight at speed.

Other ongoing tyre issues for race teams are the ideal hardness of the tread, which can vary depending on the surface or temperature of the day's race, and the ideal tyre width in terms of both surface performance and aerodynamics.

The big names to have supplied tyres to successful Tour riders include Hutchinson, Mavic and Continental, but the winning tyre used by Bradley Wiggins in 2012 was the Veloflex Record, a 180-gram lightweight handmade in Italy by the relatively small Veloflex company.

Cycling Apparel

Cycling apparel has become every bit as 'space age' as the bike and its components, but today's concern over whether a rider's go-faster clothing conforms to UCI rules was not exactly an issue for the earlier Tour de France riders. Let us turn the clock back for a few moments to the golden age of wool.

Woolly Riders

Throughout the early decades of the race, jerseys were made from wool, as no synthetic fibres existed which had both the warmth and the absorption of sheep's wool. Riders added the name of the team for which they were riding by attaching a panel of printed cloth to the front of the jersey with pins. Embroidery was expensive and so the only lettering to appear on the yellow jersey were the initials of Henri Desgrange.

Synthetic thread and blends were added in 1947, following the arrival of Sofil as a sponsor. Sofil made artificial yarn, which they used to produce the yellow jerseys for the race. Little did they realise the crisis that would develop when they tried to award one to the Frenchman Louison Bobet…

A Stitch in Time...

Louison Bobet was the first rider to win three consecutive Tours (1953–1955). But he was also known as a bit of a crybaby, and the French press lambasted him for it. One of the things he obsessed about was personal hygiene, and he considered pure wool to be the only material hygienic enough for a bike rider. So when Sofil presented him with a yellow jersey, he refused to wear it on account of its artificial yarn content. Sofil arranged for someone to work through the night to produce a pure wool version, and the crisis was averted.

High Fashion

Sofil may have been hurt by Monsieur Bobet's ingratitude in 1947, but they did start a trend that has since blossomed into the multimillion-pound worldwide cycle clothing industry that we see today. Little could they have anticipated the move through the early rayon, nylon and viscose materials of the fifties and sixties to the water-repellent, mesh-ventilated, moisture-transferring, sun-protecting materials of today, like micro-grid polyester with added night vision.

Nowadays even the very biggest British names get in on the act. British fashion icon Paul Smith, whose own cycling ambitions were cut short after a dreadful cycling accident when he was still a teenager, designed limited-edition Rapha jerseys to commemorate the start of the 2007 Tour in London.

Le Coq Sportif has supplied the *maillot jaune* since 1951 and the French bank, Crédit Lyonnais (now LCL), has sponsored it since 1987, along with the cuddly toy lion – *le lion en peluche* – that is handed out to each stage winner of the Tour. Advertising on race jerseys has appealed to an ever-increasing range of sponsors down the years, from the big-name brands like Ford, Mars and Peugeot to the initially not-quite-so-well-known providers of anti-snoring products (Silence) and burritos (Chipotle). We will come back to sponsorship when we get to the Tour 'caravan' in the chapter headed 'The Race'.

The Helmet Issue

Many of the European riders originally wore 'skid-lids' made of leather strips, not much use in a direct impact but they probably saved a few cuts along the way. Fausto Coppi was ridiculed for wearing one on the instructions of his wife after his brother had died from head injuries sustained during a bike crash in 1951.

Non-European riders preferred to look cool in cloth caps and Americans thought it would be even cooler to turn theirs round so that their heads looked as if they were on back to front, thereby spawning one of the great fashion disasters of the twentieth century. At least, in this way, the backs of their necks were protected from the sun, even if their heads were left to do unprotected battle with concrete.

Although technology brought polystyrene shell helmets as early as the 1970s, on the way to the thinner, lighter, more breathable, carbon fibre helmets we see today, it would be 2003 before helmets became compulsory in the Tour. Not even the death of Fabio Casartelli on the descent of the Col de Portet d'Aspet in 1995 (see the section 'Troubles and Tragedies' in the chapter headed 'The Race' for more detail) convinced the riders that they needed to protect themselves.

In 2003 Tour riders were allowed the one exception of removing their helmets before the final climb of a mountaintop finish, resulting in the bizarre spectacle of the whole field chucking their helmets in the general direction of their team helpers. The exception was ended by 2005.

Nowadays, of course, helmets are not only desired by Tour riders for reasons of personal safety, they also provide crucial time gains on account of their streamlined design, not to mention sponsorship opportunities. One American rider has even been heard saying that he thought a Kask Bambino TT helmet was cooler than a back-to-front baseball cap.

Chapter 5
Training for Le Tour

> '*To prepare for a race there is nothing better than a good pheasant, some champagne and a woman.*'
>
> **Jacques Anquetil**

Jacques Anquetil's idea of race preparation back in the swinging sixties sounds like a lot of fun compared to today's somewhat stricter regimes. But even Anquetil's regime of pheasant, champagne and a member of the opposite sex would have seemed unnecessarily sophisticated to the early Tour riders, often photographed with a cigarette hanging from the corner of their mouth and a hip flask of cognac in their shorts (for medicinal pain-killing purposes only, you understand). The only training to be had back then involved riding your bike whenever you got the chance and it probably wasn't even called 'training'.

Those early 'training regimes' were a far cry from today's purpose-built training camps on a sunny Mediterranean island, or nestled in the Tuscan hills, complete with on-site chefs and masseurs. Whole teams ride together, live together, eat together and play together. Thanks to modern communications media, fans can even follow their every training move in between races. If you want to see pictures of this morning's training ride, or know what Fabian Cancellara had for breakfast, or what Mark Cavendish thinks of his room-mate (who, incidentally, was his best mate, the Austrian Bernie Eisel, for five whole years until Cavendish left Eisel behind at Team Sky in late 2012), just log on to the team's website or follow the tweets of your favourite rider.

Pass the Bubbly!

At the start of the fourteenth stage in the 1964 Tour, Jacques Anquetil was being dropped by his great rival, Raymond Poulidor. Anquetil put this down to indigestion after attending a lamb barbecue 'training session' on the preceding rest day, and decided to reinvigorate himself with a bottle of champagne supplied by his team manager. After taking the bubbly on board, he was immediately back on form. Poulidor was caught and Anquetil went on to win his fifth consecutive Tour.

Nowadays, being in peak condition for the Tour requires careful planning, and you have to mix the right training schedule with the right racing schedule. Unless you are an Eddy Merckx clone (in which case, just turn up and win anyway), you need to be just the right amount of 'match fit' when you line up at the start of the Tour and you don't want to be carrying any niggling injuries if you can help it. If that means missing out on some of the early-season Classics or even the Giro d'Italia, then so be it, if your focus is to enter the record books of the greatest cycle race on earth.

Riding High

It has been suggested that a GC rider climbs the equivalent of 100,000 vertical metres in preparation for a Tour. If he did this vertically in one go (and I'm not suggesting for one minute that this would be a sensible thing to do), he would be at the top of Mount Everest after just 8,848 of those metres. At 11,887 metres he would be waving to aeroplane passengers, and at 85,000 metres he would have entered the mesosphere, which is where meteors heading for earth tend to burn up. L'Alpe d'Huez must seem like a molehill after that.

So what exactly do you have to do to become a lean, mean twenty-first-century Tour fighting machine, to be just the right amount of lean to maximise your strength-to-weight ratio and minimise your own drag, but not sacrifice power in the process? Here is a checklist of the kinds of things you might work on:

- Find out your ideal riding weight and adhere to the right diet to achieve it without sacrificing nutritional benefit.
- Build a base position with low-intensity workouts (but bear in mind that a Tour rider's low-intensity level may be higher than your normal high-intensity level and adjust to Tour level accordingly – if in doubt, just double your normal workout intensity).
- Spend your winters in warm-weather training camps.
- Ride a lot of long climbs at close to your threshold power output of 6.7 watts per kilogram of body weight. Three repetitions of 25-minute climbs in 35-degree heat is the sort of thing you might try for starters.
- Carry out a strength and conditioning programme at the gym to develop core muscles that cycling alone can't reach.
- Put a lot of miles in at high pedal cadences, either on flat roads or in the gym, to maximise your anaerobic capacity for the time trials in particular.
- Get some altitude. Ideally you want to sleep at altitude while training at various heights at and above sea level. So ride up and down mountains during the day but make sure you sleep at the top every night.

- If you can't make it to Tenerife or Mallorca, buy an oxygen tent for the spare room and train in an altitude centre (there's one in Putney).

- Spend time in a wind tunnel to determine the ideal aerodynamic position for your particular metabolism (you might not actually function that well in the position that offers your particular body the least amount of drag, so it's not as simple as you might think to get this right).

- Get a sports psychologist to convince you that you can't be beaten.

- Take your recovery time seriously – don't stand when you can sit; don't sit when you can lie down; avoid stairs like the plague.

- You're good to go.

A Strange Case of Climacophobia

As far as I'm aware, five-times Tour winner Bernard Hinault didn't have a fear of climbing stairs (climacophobia), but he did allegedly worry about the effect that climbing or descending stairs would have on his racing muscles. In fact, he worried to the extent that he would have his soigneurs carry him up and down them whenever he was entering or leaving a hotel.

Tour de France DIY

If you want to simulate Tour race conditions in your own indoor training regime, simply fork out about £1,500 for a decent twenty-four-gear digital-console training bike with automatic tilt mechanism and use the software supplied to create your own 'authentic' Tour stage. Set up your training bike to mirror your real one and you're off. Feel every French incline and decline as if you were there and feel just the right amount of wind thanks to the 'intelligent wind resistance' you have factored in according to your own height and weight and riding-style profiles.

And just one last training-related tip before we leave this chapter behind: don't forget to be born with the right genes in the first place, because it takes more than the best training regime ever devised to win the Tour de France. If you just don't have a physiology that can take superman-level training in its stride, that can take on board extra oxygen and pump blood faster than that of an ordinary mortal, I'm afraid you're doomed to something less than cycling glory anyway. Try football, maybe.

Chapter 6
The Race

'You don't suffer, kill yourself and take the risks I take just for the money. I love bike racing.'

Greg LeMond, American three-times Tour winner

In this chapter we will look at the race from a lot of different angles, including those of the race organisers, the myriad sponsors, the media, the police, the logistics people and, of course, the spectator. But, because the Tour de France is first and foremost a bike race, we will begin by pondering the question of what it must look and feel like from on board one of the bikes. ('Very scary' is the short answer.)

➤ In the Saddle

'There will be a lot of complaining that today was too hard, but the winners never complain.'

Phil Liggett, iconic Tour de France commentator

Velocity

The first thing you might notice if you suddenly found yourself in the middle of a Tour de France stage is the speed at which you seem to be travelling – seriously fast! In fact, you are probably not going to have a lot of time to enjoy the scenery, however magnificent it might be, because as well as going seriously fast, you're going to have to watch where you're going. Whether you're in the middle of the main bunch at forty kilometres an hour (25 mph) riding millimetres from the wheel you are following and centimetres from the handlebars to either side of you, or taking a hairpin bend at speed on the way down a mountainside which promises a sheer drop over the edge if you get it slightly wrong, or swerving to avoid screaming, boozed-up spectators who are running up the mountain beside you to get on the telly for as long as it takes for them to burn out (about ten seconds is normal), you are going to have to keep your wits about you.

!✱?# **Colourful Language** You're also going to have to get used to some pretty unusual noises if you're new to this whole 'racing at speed with two hundred other guys' thing. In the middle of the peloton, for example, the number of languages simultaneously shouting warnings and instructions against a continuous background noise of moving mechanical parts and screaming spectators might surprise you. Unless, of course, strong crosswinds on an open road are buffeting your ears, in which case you won't be able to hear yourself think.

> *'Learn to swear in different languages.*
> *Other riders will appreciate your*
> *efforts to communicate.'*

Robert Millar, Scottish winner of the King of the Mountains Classification, on how to fit into the peloton

Close Encounters There are two noises you really don't want to hear, though. One is the apparent explosion of the peloton that you're riding in. You might be able to hear the crunching of bikes and bodies a split second before you see them, and you might be able to see them a split second before you join them, but join them you will, as will the riders behind who are going to land on top of you. If you're lucky, your bike will come off worse than your bones and you may be able to rejoin the race, with or without your collarbone intact, on one of the spare bikes being carried by your team car. The second noise you want to avoid is the sudden, deafening 'whoosh' of the peloton swallowing you up and spitting you out the back in a matter of seconds after you have spent a couple of hours in a courageous, punishing breakaway, hoping beyond hope that you are going to upset all the odds and hold out for the unlikeliest of stage victories.

Pain!
Notwithstanding all this noise and speed and constant danger, you are also going to have to focus on what your body is doing, not least during the periods when it's squealing

at your brain to please, for the love of God, just make the pain stop. There will be times, especially on the tougher climbs, when your heart feels like it's going to explode out of your chest, when lactic acid has seeped all the way to your fingertips and eyelids, and when your muscles feel like they might snap apart. In order to manage your body's more rebellious tendencies at times like these, you are going to have to give it exactly the right amount of food (i.e. nutrient-rich gel packs) and exactly the right amount of water at exactly the right intervals, because a few hundred millilitres too little or too much can make the difference between winning the stage and watching the guy in front winning the stage.

You are also going to have to keep your body at the right temperature. Sometimes this will involve not getting overheated by the unforgiving summer sun. Other times it will involve sticking a spectator's newspaper down your jersey so that you don't freeze on your way down the mountain that you just sweated like a pig to get up. If your body still isn't happy after all this loving care and attention, you're just going to have to get your brain to tell it to shut the hell up and get on with the one simple job it's been given – pedalling through screaming pain.

And you must never forget that all the while there is a game of poker being played, in the sense that you don't want your competitors to know how you are really feeling. When you feel excruciating pain, you must remember to look bored. When you can't breathe, you must nonchalantly close your mouth. When you are about to die, you must smile easily at your fellow riders. When they smile back, you must remember that they are about to die.

When you finally get to the end of the day's race, your body and your brain are probably going to come back together like old friends to sing a duet of joy and relief – at least until they remember that they have to get straight on an exercise bike and start pedalling (of all things) in order to 'warm down'.

If you have just won the stage or won/retained one of the coveted jerseys, you can now wander off in a euphoric state to the podium to be awarded a cuddly toy lion and a yellow or green or white or polka dot jersey and be kissed on both cheeks by two pretty young girls in yellow or green or white or polka dot dresses. Otherwise, you are now free to collapse on the team bus.

Fuel

Either way, you are probably starting to feel a bit hungry about now. The good news about this, if you're in one of the rock-star teams at least, is that delicious food of your choice is going to be expertly prepared by the team chef. The not-so-good news about this is that the team nutritionist is going to be watching to make sure that you don't exceed the number of calories and nutrients needed to replenish your body, no matter how ravenous you are. This is because the last thing you need tomorrow is an extra half-ounce of fat to haul up Mont Ventoux, and that half-ounce of fat may be the difference between meeting and not meeting tomorrow's pretty podium girls.

Santé

If breakneck speed, danger to life and limb, excruciating pain, extreme weather conditions and food rationing are not your things, don't even think about asking if you can race in the Tour. Instead, pour yourself a nice glass of cool Chablis and enjoy the rest of the chapter sitting comfortably on the body fat that you have not had to surrender to the pursuit of racing glory.

➤ Around France

'From Paris to the blue waves of the Mediterranean, from Marseille to Bordeaux, passing along the roseate and dreaming roads sleeping under the sun, across the calm of the fields of the Vendée', following the Loire, which flows on still and silent, our men are going to race madly, unflaggingly.'

Henri Desgrange, writing before the first Tour in 1903

Educating the French

In the early part of the twentieth century, French people were largely unaware of the shape of the country they lived in, far less its varied geography. Newspaper reports and maps of the Tour changed all that and gave France a national identity that it had hitherto lacked. The Tour also brought the life and excitement previously enjoyed only in big cities to France's provincial backwaters, even if only for a day.

The French Revolution

As we have seen, the French often refer to the Tour as 'La Grande Boucle' – literally 'the big buckle' – because that's exactly what it was from its inception in 1903 right the way through to 1950. In the first three years the 'boucle' was a clockwise circumference of less than 3,000 km (1,875 miles), but in 1906 it stretched out to 4,545 km (2,824 miles), and it carried on stretching towards the coastlines and land borders of France's perimeter in a seemingly desperate attempt to extend the country itself. It would achieve obese proportions of over 5,500 km (3,440 miles) in the 1920s, before putting itself on a diet that would bring it back to a more sensible 4,500 km (2,800 miles) by the time the organisers finally abandoned the idea of a circular route altogether in 1951. They simultaneously abandoned the idea that the race should ideally start in Paris, and it has rarely done so since.

In recent decades the route has settled at a positively trim average of 3,500 km (2,190 miles), but it has also managed to finally conquer every single region of France (Corsica being the last to fall in 2013), plus all of its neighbouring countries and beyond, with a series of un-geometric, and often broken, shapes. La Grande Boucle may no longer be living up to its name, but it has become increasingly interesting by not doing so.

It's All about the Route

Well, not quite. You need bikes and the best bike racers on the planet as well. But the route has a lot more influence on the race than many people might imagine. For a start, throughout the course of the Tour's history the route has influenced the number of riders who can actually reach Paris. It is no coincidence that only twenty-five out of 140 riders completed the 1913 race because 5,287 km (3,305 miles) over fifteen stages on a heavy steel bike with only one gear is going to break most men.

In 1963 the organisers reportedly tried to break the dominance of Jacques Anquetil (presumably in favour of many French people's favourite, Raymond Poulidor) by introducing shorter time trials and longer climbs.

It didn't work. But in 1989 their decision to finish the Tour with a time trial did pay huge dividends, bringing about the GC's closest and most exciting finish ever.

Nowadays a rider's chances of winning the Tour can still be strongly affected by the route, in particular by the ratio of time trials to mountain stages, and potential wearers of the yellow jersey on day two of the race are largely determined by whether day one is a prologue or a longer time trial or a flat stage with a sprint finish.

Too Much Rouge?

The final kilometre of each stage on the route is signified by the *flamme rouge*, a red triangle above the road. As the leaders spring towards the finish at the sight of this, somewhere far behind is the *lanterne rouge*, the traditional title awarded to the rider who is running last in the Tour. In the early days of the Tour, the rider in last place actually had a small red light placed under his saddle, but nowadays it is more symbolic. Finishing the entire Tour in last place does bring with it a cash prize, however, in recognition of the fact that the last rider to finish (as opposed to dropping out) has probably defied injury, illness or bad luck to do so.

'Vous êtes des assassins!'
('You are assassins!')

French rider Octave Lapize getting angry with race officials on his way up the Col d'Aubisque in 1910

It's Complicated!

The routes of today are determined up to two years in advance in order to allow sufficient time for the massive amount of planning and preparation that is needed to realise them. (You can't really be telling Leeds that it will have the privilege of hosting the start of the Tour de France in two months' time.)

The race director and his team have to take account of an ever-increasing number of factors in determining future routes. They have to get the right mix of time trials, sprints and climbs in order to ensure the variety and excitement that fans and the media have come to expect. They must take advantage of the growing interest beyond French borders – the decision to return to Britain in 2014 had everything to do with the huge success of the 2007 visit, as well as the unprecedented success of British cycling at the 2012 Tour de France and at two consecutive Olympic Games. The organisers also have to ensure that the vast logistics of any proposed route are feasible and they need to meet a whole raft of health and safety and security requirements. That means an awful lot of liaison with an awful lot of interested parties.

It almost goes without saying that the route also has to include a bewildering array of stunningly picturesque towns and villages, beautiful coastlines and lakes, breathtaking mountaintops, pleasing rural landscapes and commanding châteaux. On the surface, that seems to be the least of the organisers' worries given the geography they have to work with, but they will be lobbied and harried constantly by those who would have the prestige and glamour of the Tour passing through their village or town or département or region or even country. The greatest prize of all for those glamour-seeking lobbyists is the ultimate Tour accolade of hosting the Grand Départ, the first mass-start stage of the Tour (which normally happens on day two after a prologue or time trial on day one).

Sprinters Only, Please

Although the Points Classification usually remains up for grabs, there is a gentlemen's agreement that the GC will not be fought over on the final day's race (the race leader usually has too much time in hand to be caught on the flat in any event). The peloton will therefore enjoy a glass or two of champagne on the way into the city, although the sprinters will probably stick to water until after the final mad dash for glory on the Champs-Elysées.

To understand just how good the organisers have become at compiling a Tour de France route *par excellence*, consider the thinking that must have gone into the mouth-watering route of the 2013 Tour, the hundredth running of the race:

- Exclusively within France for the first time in ten years.

- Grand Départ in Corsica, the only region of France never to have been hitherto crossed by the Tour.

- Team time trial on the Promenade des Anglais in Nice.

- Individual time trial at Mont St Michel.

- Sprint finishes in Marseille, Montpellier, Saint-Malo and, of course, on the Champs-Elysées.

- Pyrenees and Alps for the climbers, including the epic Mont Ventoux and a double ascent of the iconic l'Alpe d'Huez.

- A final climb on the penultimate day to Le Semnoz, a ski station opposite Mont Blanc.

- Early evening departure from the Palais de Versailles to ensure a race finale in Paris under floodlights, with the usual Champs-Elysées loops extending to include the Arc de Triomphe.

A Potted History of Interesting Facts

As you may have gathered by now, it is not going to be possible to cover the detail of Tour de France routes in a book that is less than the size of a large coffee table. I therefore offer you the following potted history by way of consolation:

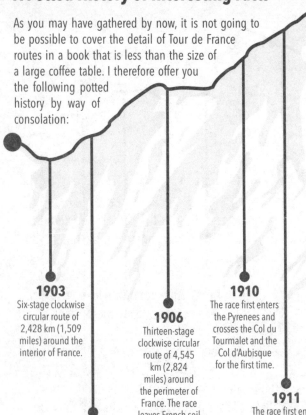

1903
Six-stage clockwise circular route of 2,428 km (1,509 miles) around the interior of France.

1905
First official mountain stage, over the Col du Ballon d'Alsace.

1906
Thirteen-stage clockwise circular route of 4,545 km (2,824 miles) around the perimeter of France. The race leaves French soil for the first time when it crosses the German border into Alsace-Lorraine. (The Germans later prohibited this after the 1910 race and the Tour retreated back inside its own borders.)

1910
The race first enters the Pyrenees and crosses the Col du Tourmalet and the Col d'Aubisque for the first time.

1911
The race first enters the Alps and crosses the Col du Galibier (Henri Desgrange's favourite mountain) for the first time. Like the Col du Tourmalet and the Col d'Aubisque, this is still a dirt road at the time.

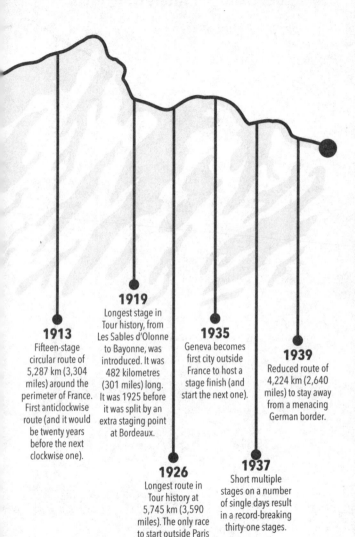

1913
Fifteen-stage circular route of 5,287 km (3,304 miles) around the perimeter of France. First anticlockwise route (and it would be twenty years before the next clockwise one).

1919
Longest stage in Tour history, from Les Sables d'Olonne to Bayonne, was introduced. It was 482 kilometres (301 miles) long. It was 1925 before it was split by an extra staging point at Bordeaux.

1926
Longest route in Tour history at 5,745 km (3,590 miles). The only race to start outside Paris (in Evian) between 1903 and 1950.

1935
Geneva becomes first city outside France to host a stage finish (and start the next one).

1937
Short multiple stages on a number of single days result in a record-breaking thirty-one stages.

1939
Reduced route of 4,224 km (2,640 miles) to stay away from a menacing German border.

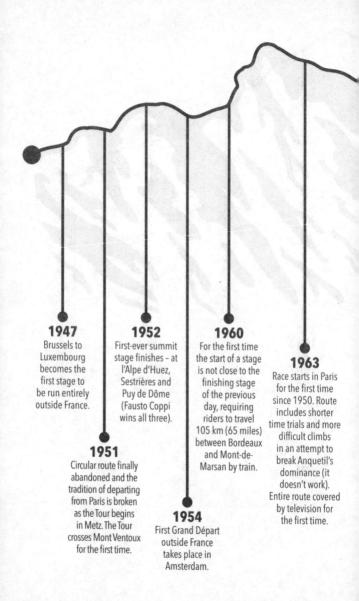

1947
Brussels to Luxembourg becomes the first stage to be run entirely outside France.

1952
First-ever summit stage finishes – at l'Alpe d'Huez, Sestrières and Puy de Dôme (Fausto Coppi wins all three).

1960
For the first time the start of a stage is not close to the finishing stage of the previous day, requiring riders to travel 105 km (65 miles) between Bordeaux and Mont-de-Marsan by train.

1963
Race starts in Paris for the first time since 1950. Route includes shorter time trials and more difficult climbs in an attempt to break Anquetil's dominance (it doesn't work). Entire route covered by television for the first time.

1951
Circular route finally abandoned and the tradition of departing from Paris is broken as the Tour begins in Metz. The Tour crosses Mont Ventoux for the first time.

1954
First Grand Départ outside France takes place in Amsterdam.

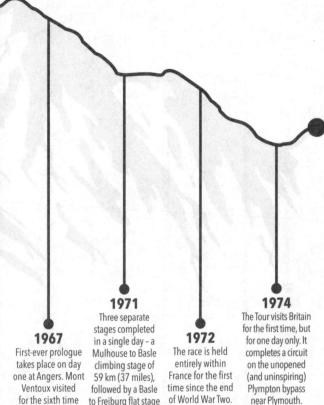

1967
First-ever prologue takes place on day one at Angers. Mont Ventoux visited for the sixth time and claims the life of British rider Tom Simpson (see the 'Troubles and Tragedies' section in this chapter for more detail).

1971
Three separate stages completed in a single day – a Mulhouse to Basle climbing stage of 59 km (37 miles), followed by a Basle to Freiburg flat stage of 90 km (56 miles) and a Freiburg to Mulhouse flat stage of 74 km (46 miles). (Two stages completed in a single day was not uncommon around this time, but three was rare.)

1972
The race is held entirely within France for the first time since the end of World War Two.

1974
The Tour visits Britain for the first time, but for one day only. It completes a circuit on the unopened (and uninspiring) Plympton bypass near Plymouth. Riders were unhappy with delays caused by British immigration officials on the way back to France. It was no surprise that the organisers did not return to Britain for the next twenty years.

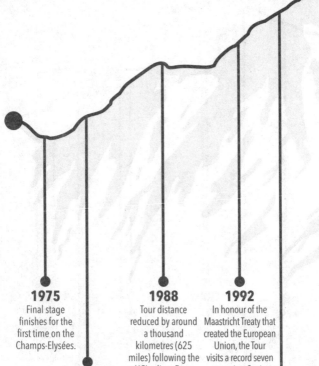

1975
Final stage finishes for the first time on the Champs-Elysées.

1987
Tour starts in West Berlin, the furthest it has ever been from French soil, and spends the first five days in West Germany. Twenty-six stages with only one rest day causes UCI ruling that major races cannot span three whole weekends.

1988
Tour distance reduced by around a thousand kilometres (625 miles) following the UCI ruling. From this point Tours will average 3,500 km (2,190 miles), normally over twenty-one stages with two rest days.

1992
In honour of the Maastricht Treaty that created the European Union, the Tour visits a record seven countries: Spain, France, Belgium, the Netherlands, Germany, Luxembourg and Italy.

1994
The Tour returns to Britain for two stages, Dover to Brighton followed by a circular route around Portsmouth.

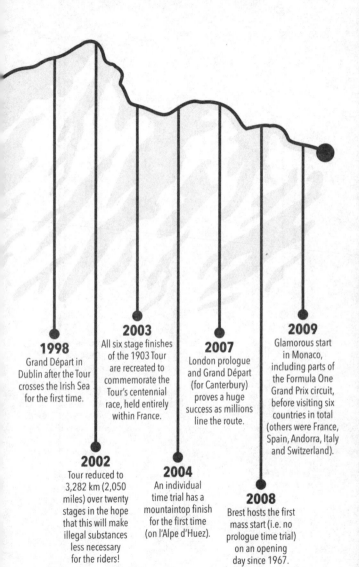

1998
Grand Départ in Dublin after the Tour crosses the Irish Sea for the first time.

2002
Tour reduced to 3,282 km (2,050 miles) over twenty stages in the hope that this will make illegal substances less necessary for the riders!

2003
All six stage finishes of the 1903 Tour are recreated to commemorate the Tour's centennial race, held entirely within France.

2004
An individual time trial has a mountaintop finish for the first time (on l'Alpe d'Huez).

2007
London prologue and Grand Départ (for Canterbury) proves a huge success as millions line the route.

2008
Brest hosts the first mass start (i.e. no prologue time trial) on an opening day since 1967.

2009
Glamorous start in Monaco, including parts of the Formula One Grand Prix circuit, before visiting six countries in total (others were France, Spain, Andorra, Italy and Switzerland).

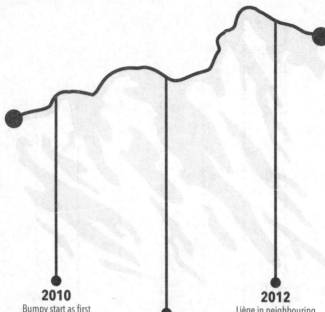

2010

Bumpy start as first three stages through the Netherlands and Belgium include a total of 13.2 km (8.2 miles) of cobblestones. Emphasis is on the Pyrenees as opposed to the Alps (with two ascents of the Col du Tourmalet) to commemorate the hundredth anniversary of the Tour's first visit to the Pyrenees in 1910.

2011

Emphasis is on the Alps as opposed to the Pyrenees to commemorate the hundredth anniversary of the Tour's first visit to the Alps in 1911. The Col du Galibier is visited twice and used as a stage finish for the first time. At 2,645 metres (8,678 feet), this is the highest summit finish in Tour history.

2012

Liège in neighbouring Belgium hosts the eighteenth Grand Départ outside of France. The Col du Tourmalet in the Pyrenees is included for a record-breaking seventy-seventh time, while the Col du Grand Colombier in the Jura Mountains is included for the first time. The Frenchman Thomas Voeckler is first over both summits, a week apart, on his way to the King of the Mountains title.

Souvenir Henri Desgrange

This €5,000 prize is awarded each year on the queen stage (the stage that includes the Tour's highest point) to the first rider over the summit of that year's highest mountain.

Epic Mountains

Mont Ventoux

In common with other epic Tour climbs, Mont Ventoux is long and steep, but it also gets battered by the brutal mistral wind (hence its name, *venteux* being French for 'windswept'). The mistral has blown away most of the vegetation and left the mountain resembling a moonscape. Its nicknames include 'the Beast of Provence' and 'the Bald Mountain'. A memorial near the summit commemorates the death of British rider Tom Simpson on the mountain during the 1967 Tour (see the 'Troubles and Tragedies' section in this chapter for more detail).

L'Alpe d'Huez

Climbing a thousand metres (3,280 feet) in just 14 kilometres (8 miles) with the help of twenty-one *virages* (hairpin bends), l'Alpe d'Huez has been an epic Tour challenge since 1952, when Fausto Coppi became the first man to the ski station at the top. His name is immortalised along with other l'Alpe d'Huez stage winners on signs around the twenty-one switchback bends. It is estimated that three hundred thousand spectators line the slopes of this mountain on race days, and that a third of them are Dutch, who just decided at some point, and for no particular reason, to make this mountain their home in the days leading up to and during a Tour visit.

Col du Tourmalet

Visited when the Tour first went to the Pyrenees in 1910 (a year before the Tour visited the Alps for the first time), and since visited by the Tour more than any other mountain, the western ascent to the Col du Tourmalet is a long, steady climb of 1,395 metres (4,576 feet) that can have a significant bearing on the outcome of the GC and King of the Mountains competitions. There is a memorial at the top to Jacques Goddet, Desgrange's successor and extrovert director of the Tour from 1936 until 1987, and a large statue of Octave Lapize gasping for air as he struggles up the climb to become the first-ever rider over the top in 1910.

Col du Galibier

First crossed when the Tour went over the Alps for the first time in 1910, the Col du Galibier is a long, hard climb that saves its steepest incline for the final push to the summit. The first man over in 1910, Emile Georget, was one of only three not to get off and push his bike through the mud and gravel that passed for the road at the time. A monument to Henri Desgrange stands at the tunnel entrance near the summit.

Col d'Aubisque

A Tour regular since it was first crossed in 1910 on the Tour's first visit to the Pyrenees, the tough climb is followed by an even harder descent of up to 13 per cent gradients and narrow hairpins. The Dutchman Wim van Est found out just how tricky it could be when he went over the edge on his way down the mountain in 1951. (You can read about his narrow escape from death in the 'Troubles and Tragedies' section of this chapter.) A memorial marks the spot where van Est went over the edge, as does a safety barrier.

Col de la Madeleine

Another Tour regular since first being crossed in 1969, the climb of this French Alp rises about fifteen hundred metres (4,921 feet) in a little over 38 kilometres (23 miles) at an average gradient of 8 per cent. Like the Col d'Aubisque, the descent is also frightening and, in a ridiculous case of déjà vu, another Dutchman (Johan van der Velde in 1981) went over the edge and narrowly escaped death by landing on a ledge just a few feet from the top.

Col du Ballon d'Alsace

The first proper mountain stage of the Tour de France, in 1905. The French rider René Pottier was first over the top. He was the only rider to remain seated all the way, and developed tendonitis for his troubles. Henri Desgrange placed a monument at the summit in Pottier's memory, after Pottier committed suicide in 1907 (reportedly because his wife had an affair while he was away winning the 1906 Tour). The Tour returned to the Ballon d'Alsace in 2005 to commemorate the centenary of the first crossing.

Hors Catégorie
(Beyond Categorisation)

Points are awarded in the King of the Mountains Classification depending on the length and steepness of the mountains being climbed. There were four categories of difficulty until a fifth, *hors catégorie*, was added in 1979 to classify the most difficult of ascents. L'Alpe d'Huez has provided the most hors catégorie climbs (twenty-three), followed by the Col du Tourmalet (twenty) and the Col du Galibier (nineteen).

Highest Tour Climbs

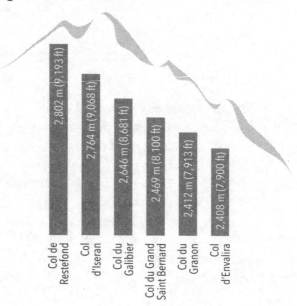

- 2,802 m (9,193 ft) — Col de Restefond
- 2,764 m (9,068 ft) — Col d'Iseran
- 2,646 m (8,681 ft) — Col du Galibier
- 2,469 m (8,100 ft) — Col du Grand Saint Bernard
- 2,412 m (7,913 ft) — Col du Granon
- 2,408 m (7,900 ft) — Col d'Envalira

Tour Favourites

The most popular cities and towns to have hosted stage starts/finishes outside of Paris (which has featured every year) are as follows:

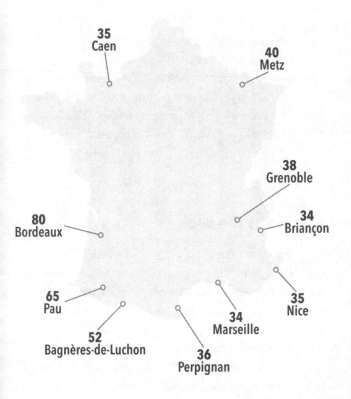

35
Caen

40
Metz

38
Grenoble

80
Bordeaux

34
Briançon

65
Pau

35
Nice

52
Bagnères-de-Luchon

34
Marseille

36
Perpignan

> *'We cannot apply the same recipe each year. We can't hit "copy and paste".'*
>
> **Christian Prudhomme, Tour de France Race Director**

L'Etape du Tour

This mock Tour stage is run annually for thousands of amateur riders who want to experience one of the stages within a couple of weeks of the actual Tour stage itself. Most of them will take several hours longer than the professional Tour riders to complete it but it will be a lot of fun and they will raise a lot of money for charity in the process.

➤ Going by the Book

The early Tour riders had to contend with the weird and wonderful, and often quite draconian rules imposed by Henri Desgrange in his attempts to ensure that the Tour was only won by men who could not be broken under extreme forms of torture. At various times he resisted clamours for multiple gears, non-wooden wheel rims, pacers for the better riders, and permission to change damaged bikes (it would be 1956 before it was allowed to even change a damaged wheel). In Desgrange's defence, he was dealing with some very naughty boys and he probably became determined to keep a handle on things after learning, as we have already seen, that widespread cheating and general skulduggery were part and parcel of the riders' behaviour in the early years.

Henri Pélissier, the 1923 champion, was forever at loggerheads with Desgrange over the rules that were imposed on the riders. He pulled out of three Tours halfway through and spurned two completely. He pulled out of the 1919 Tour because Desgrange refused him an extra glass of wine at a post-race reception. He pulled out of the 1920 Tour after Desgrange penalised him two minutes for leaving a flat tyre at the side of the road. He pulled out of the 1924 Tour in protest at a new rule that riders had to finish a stage with the same amount of clothing that they started with, even if the stage started in cooler conditions and finished in scorching heat. He also protested against strict food-rationing rules during races.

Today's rules are somewhat more reasonable. Here is a selection of those that are most likely to aid understanding of the Tour from a spectator's point of view:

- It is compulsory to wear a helmet at all times.

- Each rider must wear the designated outfit of his team unless he qualifies to wear a jersey of greater importance, e.g. the yellow jersey. If a rider leads more than one race competition, he wears the most important jersey (yellow, green, polka dot and white in that order) and the next-placed rider in the foregone classification wears that particular jersey.

- Riders can swap bikes or wheels, but only with members of their own team.

- Bikes must weigh at least 6.8 kg (15 lbs).

- Riders are allowed to take food bags (known as *musettes*) and drinks bottles on their way through official feeding stations. (Riders can also accept food and drink from spectators, but not many would risk not knowing exactly what they were being given.)

- Any rider can drop back from the peloton to get assistance from his own team car or any neutral assistance car, but this does not include holding on to the car for longer than is necessary to get the advice or medical assistance required!

- Riders are not generally allowed to take food or drink from a team or neutral assistance car within the first 50 kilometres (31.2 miles) or final 20 kilometres (12.5 miles) of a race.

- Team cars may carry spare bikes, wheels, water, food and medical supplies. During the race, the primary team vehicle must be driven by the directeur sportif on the right-hand side of the road and in the order designated at the stage start.

- Riders must finish a stage within a set cut-off time to avoid elimination from the remainder of the Tour. (Organisers have a very good idea how long each stage should reasonably take, based on experience and because they will have toured the route numerous times during the planning stage.)

- Performance-enhancing drugs and all forms of blood doping are strictly prohibited and punishable by public humiliation on *The Oprah Winfrey Show*.

Back-breaking Stuff

Frenchman Victor Fontan took two bullets in the leg during World War One, but still went on to race his first Tour in 1924 at the ripe old age of thirty-two. At the even riper age of thirty-seven, he crashed while wearing the maillot jaune in 1929. Because of the rule that you had to finish a stage with the same bike you started with, he borrowed a fresh one and rode it through the Pyrenees with the original bike strapped to his back!

The Very, Very, Nice Men from Mavic

Since 1973, the iconic yellow cars and motorcycles of bike component manufacturer, Mavic, have been providing neutral assistance to riders who find themselves remote from their team cars in times of distress. So, if a Tour rider crashes during a breakaway a long way ahead of his team, Mavic may come to the rescue with a fresh tyre, wheel or even bike. Mavic provide this service in return for the publicity they get from it (the Mavic support car has become something of an unofficial Tour mascot over the years) and the Tour organisers and teams are grateful for all the help they can get in keeping the race moving and safe. A Mavic mechanic is reckoned to take about ten seconds to replace a wheel.

Drug Testing

Every rider in the Tour is tested for banned substances prior to the race. Various cyclists are tested after each stage, according to a selection process determined before the race. Under current rules, at least 180 drug tests are given, including daily drug tests for the race leader and stage winner and six to eight cyclists selected at random throughout the field.

Tour drug tests are administered in accordance with the rules of the Union Cycliste Internationale (UCI) and the Féderation Françoise de Cyclisme (FFC), and banned-substance testing is carried out under secure and strictly monitored conditions. A specially equipped caravan is established near the finish line of every stage to transport drug samples to a secret location following the race. Drug test samples are then transported by private plane for analysis, and the results are quickly reported to Tour officials to decide on appropriate action in the case of failed tests. Failed riders have the option of insisting that their 'B' sample is tested just in case the test itself has resulted in an inappropriate outcome, but it rarely makes any difference.

Immediate disqualification from the remainder of the Tour is normally the outcome for those riders who have failed tests, and being subsequently banned from the sport for one year or longer has not been uncommon in recent times either. (For more information on drug-taking and other scandals endured by the Tour over the course of its history, see the chapter headed 'Doping and Cheating'.)

The Man for the Job

The enforcement of the Tour rules, including the anti-doping rules, falls to the race director. This has been Christian Prudhomme since 2006. In true Desgrange style, this charismatic former TV presenter has taken a firm stance against recalcitrant riders, leading to the withdrawal of the Amaury Sport Organisation (the organiser of the Tour de France) from the aegis of the UCI so that the Tour could apply its own stricter anti-doping regime. (The UCI has long been tainted with accusations of turning a blind eye to the problems of doping for fear of the adverse publicity which it undoubtedly attracts to the sport.) He also called for the Tours of the Armstrong years to have no replacement winners because it was patently clear that the problems of those years extended beyond Armstrong himself.

Rider Power

The powers that be are in a very strong position to influence a race before, during and after it takes place. They did Mark Cavendish no favours when they disqualified Mark Renshaw (Cavendish's lead-out man) for headbutting an opponent during a sprint finish in the middle of the 2010 Tour, but the reduced number of intermediate sprints they agreed for the 2011 race helped Cavendish to the Green Jersey he missed out on the previous year in spite of having been the fastest man in the race. But the authorities must know their limits. Having introduced a ban on radio communication between team managers and riders on stage 10 of the 2009 Tour, they were humiliated by a riders' go-slow for most of the stage and the intended repetition of the experiment on stage 13 had to be abandoned. (Some purist officials argue that riders should not be helped by tactical advice during the race; riders and team managers see it as an integral part of modern racing.)

A Man's Gotta Do What a Man's Gotta Do

There's an unwritten rule that riders won't seek to take advantage of a roadside toilet break. (A number of riders will typically stop together on a quiet stretch of road, as they're not allowed to pee *en masse* in front of spectators.) The same unwritten rule applies whenever a rider has to have a more private moment in the bushes.

If time is of the essence, three or four riders link together to allow the man on the inside to have a pee without stopping. It is very important to take account of wind direction in manoeuvres of this nature!

The Broom Wagon

The *voiture balai* ('broom wagon') is a van that brings up the rear of the Tour every day. It is the last thing you want to see if you are a rider because it hovers like a vulture waiting to scoop up the injured and the sick and the weak. The rules state that your numbers have to be removed and handed over as you get into the van (originally designed to stop the riders getting back out and continuing the race later on). The windows are tinted to avoid spectators witnessing the shame of it all and the driver will kindly drop the failed riders off at a safe distance from the finishing line of the day's race. But more and more riders are shunning the tradition nowadays, preferring instead the comfort and reduced ignominy of travelling to the end in the team car if they are unable to continue by bike.

❯ Logistics

It is nothing short of a logistical marvel that the moving feast that is the Tour de France seems to run like clockwork across approximately 3,500 kilometres (2,190 miles) of France (and usually some of its neighbouring countries) over a three-week period year after year after year. This could not happen without dedicated organisers, several thousand people who are expert in their chosen fields, a lot of money, and the will of the French people, who happily hand over their roads and towns and villages according to the Tour's needs.

In addition to the huge entourages and vast amounts of equipment (e.g. bikes!) required by each of the twenty-one or so Tour teams, there are the hordes of ever-present journalists and TV presenters and technicians (and the cameras, sound equipment, scaffolding, press rooms and everything else they need to cover the race). Then there are the telecommunications providers, and the vehicles and personnel of the publicity caravan, the security operation and the emergency services. And then there are the trucks and drivers and assemblers needed for the nightly dismantling and rebuilding of 'Finish' and 'Start' villages up to hundreds of kilometres apart. And that's before you even get to thinking about the catering and toilet facilities for that many people.

The ubiquitous Norbert Dentressangle (if you've ever driven on French roads, you will know that Norbert Dentressangle is the French equivalent of Eddie Stobart) has been the transport provider for the Tour's 'villages' for the past thirty years. They provide a dedicated fleet of almost forty trucks and over fifty drivers moving all of the equipment needed for the 'Start' and 'Finish' villages of each stage, including security barriers, signage, advertising boards, the official Tour shop, the presentation podium, the timekeeping unit, the finishing arch and the compounds for riders, journalists and sponsors. This is a far cry from 1903, when a few pieces of chalk were all that were needed to draw the starting and finishing lines of each stage.

If you live in a French town or village and suddenly wake up in the middle of the night to a prolonged thunder that appears to be shaking your house to its very foundations, it probably just means that the Tour is on its way to wherever that morning's start point happens to be. (You will find more detailed information about the impressive logistics of the publicity caravan, the security operation and the media in the next three sections.)

▶ The 'Caravan'

La caravane du Tour, or publicity caravan, is a colourful, noisy carnival of motorised floats that precedes each stage of the Tour. The caravan was created in 1930 to help keep the Tour coffers full as Desgrange saw this general merchandise advertising as a way of keeping bicycle manufacturers at bay. As we have seen, he lived in constant fear that the latter would try to dictate the terms of his race if they were allowed to sponsor teams and he had therefore replaced them with national teams for the 1930 race, which left him needing to find more inventive ways of funding the Tour.

The few companies who formed the first caravan included La Vache Qui Rit ('The Laughing Cow' spreading cheese that is France's answer to Dairylea) and the Menier chocolate manufacturer, who threw half a million *gendarme* hats bearing their brand name into the crowd. Today over thirty brands spend up to €500,000 each for the privilege of decorating vehicles in weird and wonderful ways and throwing free goodie bags to the hyped-up spectators who line the route and scream at the passing sponsors for snacks and toys and funny hats. Imagine a giant yellow polystyrene cockerel astride a little Citroën 2CV, or suddenly getting hit in the face by a key ring thrown from a lorry by an overexcited student, and you start to get the picture.

Here are a few statistics to give you a better idea of what's involved:

180 vehicles

600 'caravanists', including drivers, mechanics and youngsters (often students) employed to chuck the gifts out

20-kilometre-long procession

45 minutes to pass through (this is about forty-four minutes and fifty seconds longer than it will take the peloton to pass you in two hours' time, so do try to enjoy it)

16 million gifts given away by the thirty brands represented over the three-week period (that's about 40,000 gifts per 'chucker-outer')

12 members of the Republican Guard for security (presumably against anti-capitalism protesters?)

4 traffic police motorcyclists to prevent spectators being run over by the caravan (hasn't always been entirely successful, though)

3 medical cars (to transport first-aiders specially trained in patching up faces mutilated by key rings)

➤ Securing the Race

Three different forces are involved in the policing of the Tour de France:

- **The Police Nationale** (responsible for security and law enforcement within cities and large towns)
- **The Gendarmerie** (which is the branch of the French military that has responsibility for security and law enforcement in more rural and border areas)
- **The Garde Républicaine** (whose normal responsibilities include guarding the president and visiting heads of state)

Nine thousand policemen and twelve thousand gendarmes do their respective things as the Tour passes through their areas of jurisdiction, but it is the forty-five motorcyclists of the Republican Guard who travel with the Tour. They live, eat and sleep the Tour for the whole three-week period. There are two support lorries: one for their luggage, which also has a washing machine, and the other to serve as a mobile mechanical support unit.

Each day brings its own issues, from overheating tarmac that is in danger of melting, to drunken spectators lining the mountain roads; from race sabotage by protesters who have thrown tacks on the road, to a publicity caravan that is not staying far enough ahead of the race. The captain in charge of the Republican Guard riders will stay ahead of the race in the control car and keep the forty-five members of his team advised of what lies ahead. His most difficult moments will involve issuing instructions to his team while holding on for dear life on mountain descents, as the control car must go fast enough to stay ahead of the lightning-fast Tour riders who refuse to shrink in the car's rear-view mirrors.

When the race leaves French soil, the Republican Guards go with it, but only to liaise with the police forces of the foreign country concerned. They will have no jurisdiction over the race while it is outside France and they must leave their guns at the border.

❯ Media Circus

The Tour de France is one of sport's great events for the media. It promises speed, excitement, triumph, tragedy and glamour, not to mention scandal of soap-opera proportions, against the most scenic of backgrounds – and it never fails to deliver. So it is little wonder that media coverage over the years has taken advantage of every technological development available.

It has moved on from the few reporters who wrote up the story for Henri Desgrange's *L'Auto* newspaper, through the excitement of the live radio broadcasts that began in the 1930s and the fuzziness of the first live television broadcast of the finish in 1948, to the living, breathing, on-the-spot images captured today from every possible vantage point and from every conceivable angle.

And these images and the stories behind them are being followed by worldwide audiences in increasingly different ways. What would the staunch traditionalist Monsieur Desgrange have made of high-definition helicopter shots being watched on mobile phones and wireless computers, or up-to-the-minute Twitter feeds as the race progresses? Here are some rough statistics that bring home the extent of twenty-first-century Tour coverage:

50,000,000 TV viewers at peak periods, and over three billion in cumulative terms over the three weeks of the race

250 TV cameramen capturing the race from purpose-built platforms, motorcycles and helicopters

120 TV channels showing coverage in almost 190 countries

60 TV channels broadcasting live

6,000,000 hits on the Tour website over the three-week period of the race

650,000 followers on the Mark Cavendish Twitter account

120,000 followers on the Tour de France Twitter account

2,500 media accreditations for journalists, photographers and cameramen

450 places provided every day in temporary press rooms for print journalists

72 radio stations

Liggett and Sherwen

For many television viewers and radio listeners around the world, the Tour de France would just not be the same without iconic commentators Phil Liggett and Paul Sherwen. There are two reasons for this. Firstly, they know their stuff. What they don't know about the Tour de France probably isn't worth knowing. Secondly, they are brilliant at what they do, which is to tell you what is happening in a relaxed, informative and often humorous way. They make it all sound so easy, but they are taking a lot more in their relaxed stride than you might imagine.

What you don't see is them switching constantly between the countries and networks they are addressing. When the NBC Sports Network is up, American interests have to take precedence, especially as the Americans are the main paymasters. When the international feed is on, they will know to let the South Africans know how Robbie Hunter is doing and tell the Australians how Cadel Evans is shaping up. When the race is starting in Europe, they will be advising Australian viewers to settle down for the evening with a nice bottle of Bottom's Creek, while apologising to the West Coast of America that it's the middle of the night, but that it's a race that looks worth sticking matchsticks in your eyes for.

And lest you think that one without the other would be like Morecambe without Wise, like Tom without

Jerry, even their apparent double act is achieved with smoke and mirrors, because they will often be addressing different parts of the world at the same time. They don't spend the rest of the year together either. For one thing, Sherwen lives in Kampala, Uganda, where he has interests in a gold mine, and Liggett spends a lot of time in South Africa, where he has a game farm on the edge of the Kruger National Park.

Honorary Frenchmen

Another illusion that Phil Liggett and Paul Sherwen manage to pull off is an encyclopaedic knowledge of every landmark that the Tour passes. In actual fact, the 'race bible' that they use is produced by the French Tourist Board, who don't generally like to hand it out to anyone who isn't French, but Liggett and Sherwen are exceptionally allowed a copy between them.

'The Sherwenator'

As a professional rider, Paul Sherwen completed the Tour de France five times. Never in with a chance of scooping the prizes, he nonetheless secured a reputation as a very tough competitor. On the first day in the mountains of the 1985 Tour, Sherwen crashed within the first kilometre. With the great Bernard Hinault setting a fast pace ahead, he had little chance to catch up. He rode solo for six hours over six mountains, with only a motorcycle outrider for company, and finished over an hour behind the stage winner, and 23 minutes outside the cut-off – the Tour publicity caravan had started its return journey down the mountain and had to move to one side to allow Sherwen to complete the stage. His courage and endurance were rewarded by reinstatement (strictly speaking, a rider should be eliminated after missing the cut-off time), which allowed him to go on and finish a fifth Tour. This is a man who understands what the Tour de France is all about.

Liggettisms

The Colemanballs of the cycling world are attributed to Phil Liggett as 'Liggettisms'. Here are a few personal favourites:

" To wear the yellow jersey is to mingle with the gods of cycling. "

" The peloton is passing a field of white cows. This region of France is known for its bovine… of course, none of that matters to any of the riders, except that they might like a nice steak at the end of the day. "

" He looks between his legs and sees nobody there! "

" Having been robbed of the day's prize, you'll notice the big sprinters aren't at the front sharpening their legs. "

" We are now deep into the intestines of the Alps. "

" He's riding that bike like a sprocket heading for the moon, which is not a place, it's a planet, and he's riding to that star. "

" He'll have to reach into his suitcase of courage! "

" He's dancing on his pedals in a most immodest way. "

Celebrity Cyclists

As professional cycling has increased globally in the last ten years, its top riders have enjoyed enhanced celebrity status. This enhanced celebrity means more opportunities to endorse everything from bikes to shampoo. Italian cycling superstars Ivan Basso and Vincenzo Nibali have been filmed stir-frying a SIDI cycling shoe in a wok, while Mark Cavendish has appeared in the shower massaging Head & Shoulders Active Sport into his scalp because it apparently gives him the cool head he needs to keep his mind on track. Alberto Contador was so rested by his FLEX mattress that he immediately jumped on his bike to climb the Tourmalet, taking the opportunity to infer through the power of advertising that he was wrongly convicted of doping after testing positive the day before he climbed the Tourmalet in the 2010 Tour. And Bradley Wiggins carried the art of advertising off as well as anyone as he climbed mountain roads on his bike alongside a running rugby league superstar Sam Tomkins, in order to announce the first live match of the season on Sky Sports.

❯ Faithful Spectators

It is estimated that fifteen million spectators line the Tour route over the three-week period of the race, and that these spectators often travel over a hundred kilometres to their chosen vantage points. What they see when they get there is very much determined by the type of stage that is taking place.

If the stage is a time trial, they will see each rider, or each team of nine riders in the case of a team time trial, speed past them at approximately two-minute intervals.

If the stage is a regular flat one, they may see a breakaway group going past up to an hour before the peloton, then the peloton itself (which will be breathtakingly brief) followed by any stragglers who are not managing to keep up with the day's pace. If they are lucky, they may be positioned near the end of the stage, in which case, as long as they don't blink, they might get to see a superfast sprint finish at the head of the peloton. They may even get to witness one of the spectacular crashes that are prone to happen at this point of the race (and,  if they do, they will probably go home with mixed feelings about what they have seen).

If, however, they have chosen to line

one of the mountain roads (and many of them will have set up their tents and campervans several days in advance to get the best vantage points), they will see an altogether slower-moving affair. The riders will be strung out, from the GC contenders playing cat and mouse games with one another up at the front to the so-called *autobus* at the back that will include the specialist sprinters, whose only desire is to finish the stage within the cut-off time. This spectating position on the mountain also affords their best opportunity to get on the telly and irritate the hell out of the riders, both of which they can achieve by running uphill alongside the riders for a few seconds.

The Red Devil

Dieter 'Didi' Senft is an obsessive German cycling fan known since 1993 as 'the Red Devil' on account of his manic jumping and running on Tour roads in a red devil costume, and his painting of trident symbols on the road some miles before he appears. He is also an inventor who has created over a hundred bicycles, including the largest mobile quint bike (bicycle built for five) that is a world-record breaking 14.8 m long and 4.2 m high.

Whatever their chosen vantage point, spectators spend an average of six hours at the side of the road waiting for the action to happen. This explains the popularity of the publicity caravan, because, as we all know, time passes much more quickly when happy, smiling youngsters are throwing things at us from the tops of elaborately decorated lorries.

It Takes All Sorts

Incroyable!

Attention-seeking Tour spectators add to the fun of the occasion in a weird and wonderful variety of costumes and, in some cases, non-costumes. Cowboys and indians (some on horseback), mankini-wearing Borats, Santa Clauses, streakers, cheerleaders, sailors, mediaeval knights and chickens, they all end up on the telly if they position themselves at the side of the road as the riders are passing.

Perhaps the luckiest spectators of the Tour are those who just happen to live in (or temporarily find themselves in) a small village or rural community that the Tour is going to pass through anyway. They get to watch the greatest race on earth without going anywhere. All they have to do is decorate their villages and fields (and a lot of them go to extraordinary lengths to do so), fill their picnic hampers with local charcuterie, *fromages* and wines, and join the all-day party at the end of their road/field/garden.

At the other end of the scale altogether, there are those who fork out €1,000 to follow the race alongside celebrities and VIPs in the pursuing motorcade, or who spend €7,500 for a helicopter view of miniature riders on miniature bikes climbing up miniature hairpin bends.

But lest I leave you here with the impression that spectating at the Tour de France is by necessity a fleeting and trivial thing, let me assure you that those who take their Tour spectating seriously are among the most knowledgeable sports fans on earth. Those who understand the complexities of the race, who understand about the competitions within the competition, who take their own cycling seriously, they see things that the casual spectator does not. They know intricate stuff like this:

- The shape of the peloton (e.g. bunch, echelon, single file) is determined by wind direction and the GC contenders are tucked into the 'arrow' at the front to stay sheltered and out of trouble.

- In a peloton bunch finish, all riders get the same time (the finishing time is only broken if there is a 'real break' between riders), although there may still be sprint or climbing points up for grabs for the riders involved in those classifications.

- Riders who crash or suffer punctures or mechanical problems within three kilometres of the finish of a stage will be awarded the same time as the finishing pack ahead (except in mountain finishes and time trials).

- What the likelihood is of a particular breakaway of riders being caught by the peloton.

- Who the sprinters are, who is going to be strong up the mountain, who is in contention for the GC.

- In a mass of almost two hundred riders, who is riding which bikes for which teams.

- Who the French riders are!

❯ Troubles and Tragedies

The Tour de France has taken lives and been responsible for a great many injuries. It has also witnessed a great number of completely unnecessary incidents and accidents caused by abject carelessness or wilful stupidity.

Deaths

ADOLPHE HÉLIÈRE

Given the dangers that Tour de France riders face, it is a ludicrous fact that the first rider to die during the course of a Tour was fatally stung by a jellyfish in the sea off Nice. This happened to the Frenchman while he was swimming during a rest day on the 1910 Tour.

FRANCISCO CEPEDA

In 1935 the Spaniard broke his skull and died after crashing at high speed and plunging down a ravine during a descent of the Col du Galibier. The crash was caused by one of his tyres peeling off the wheel rim.

TOM SIMPSON

The first British rider ever to wear the coveted yellow jersey (in stage 12 of the 1962 Tour), the popular Tom Simpson ended up being remembered as much for the manner of his death as anything else. He collapsed and died on Mont Ventoux during the 1967 Tour, after refusing to give up on the point of outright exhaustion. An autopsy revealed the cause of death to be a fatal mix of heat, brandy and amphetamines on top of a stomach upset that he had been carrying for a few days. Despite the controversy surrounding his drug-taking, he was and still is held in high regard on account of his dogged determination and will to win. A memorial stands near the spot where he died and has become something of a pilgrimage for cyclists.

FABIO CASARTELLI

The Italian Olympic gold medallist was involved in a crash at 85 kilometres an hour (53 mph) on the descent of the Col de Portet d'Aspet on stage 15 of the 1995 Tour. He died after his head struck the concrete safety blocks along the side of the road and there was much debate over whether he would have survived had he been wearing a helmet at the time.

Other deaths have included a radio reporter and his driver when they came off their motorbike into a ravine in the Pyrenees; an elderly race official struck by French sprinter André Darrigade in the Parc des Princes; two children run over by the Tour's publicity caravan; and a woman hit by a police motorcycle. The highest single death toll was twenty, after a Tour supply van hit a bridge in the Dordogne region.

Common Injuries

'Next time you are in a car travelling at forty miles per hour, think about jumping out – naked. That's what it's like when we crash.'

David Millar, Scottish five-times Tour stage winner

If you think the worst thing about a three-week slog around France is that your legs are going to hurt with all that pedalling, consider the following list of common injuries that Tour riders will inevitably have to contend with at some point or another:

Road rash: Caused by coming off your bike and scraping bits of your anatomy on concrete, stones or gravel.

Saddle sores: Caused by the constant rubbing of one particular area of your anatomy on the saddle, hour after hour, day after day.

Broken collarbone: Broken anything and everything, actually, but the collarbone seems to snap more than any other bone when riders are involved in crashes.

Back pain: Speaks for itself, really. One of the main reasons for taking masseurs on the team coach.

Heat exhaustion: Summer in the south of France can feel very hot, especially if you grew up in the British Isles.

Numb hands: It can get pretty cold at the top of a mountain at any time of the year, especially when freezing fog closes in on you.

Colds and flu: The law of averages is such that some riders are going to come down with a cold or flu attack over the course of a three-week period, and the only remedy is to grin and bear it if you want to get to Paris.

Incidents and Accidents

Sometimes accidents just happen, but they seem to 'just happen' an awful lot in the Tour de France. As does human stupidity. Here is a random selection of bizarre incidents and accidents over the years:

Backing the Favourite

The second Tour de France in 1904 saw scenes of violence when supporters of a regional favourite, Antoine Fauré, attacked his opponents as the race passed through the Loire département. Fauré was leading the stage when some two hundred of his fans tried to stop the rest of the cyclists from following him. The situation was only solved after race officials fired shots in the air, but not before one of Fauré's rivals had to give up with broken fingers! Further on, nails and broken glass had been spread along the road, which caused many flat tyres. Because of this help, Fauré was the first on top of the Col de la République, but he was overtaken later. The organisers did not return to the Loire area until 1950.

Eye, Eye!

Honoré Barthélémy lost an eye during the 1920 Tour and later had it replaced with a glass one. After winning a stage the following year, he was clapped on the back so vigorously that the glass eye flew out. He was heard to complain that he spent more on replacement eyes than he won in prize money.

The Great Escape

Wim van Est is remembered as the first Dutchman to wear the yellow jersey, and for falling into a ravine while wearing it. On a descent of the Col d'Aubisque during stage 13 of the 1951 Tour, van Est was rounding a bend when he slipped on wet gravel and went over the edge. After rolling down twenty metres, he landed in a seated position on a small flat area the size of a chair seat. One metre either side of this flat piece and he would have continued straight down for several hundred metres before hitting solid rock. As the towrope on the team car was not long enough to reach him, forty spare racing tyres were tied together and he was hauled to safety on the end of them, bruised and hurting, but with not a single bone broken.

Vive la France! (At All Costs)

In 1975 Eddy Merckx became the victim of violence when, on the climb up to Puy de Dôme on stage 14, a French spectator jumped out of the crowd and punched him on the kidney. At the time many Frenchmen, including this one obviously, were upset at the prospect of Merckx winning a sixth Tour, as that would have put the Belgian ahead of French five-times winner Jacques Anquetil. Merckx never really recovered from the incident and finished the Tour second, behind French rider Bernard Thévenet. The only consolation for Merckx was that he recognised his assailant at the top of the summit and had him arrested.

Say 'fromage'!

Stage 1 in 1994 was a relatively flat race that came down to a bunch sprint. As the riders were speeding towards the finish line, a half-witted policeman stood out from the barriers to take a photograph of the oncoming spectacle, causing the Belgian rider Wilfried Nelissen to slam straight into him while also taking out the French rider Laurent Jalabert. Other riders quickly joined them on the tarmac as they swerved and braked to no avail. Jalabert and Nelissen were forced to drop out of the race due to the serious injuries they sustained. Nelissen's injuries included a broken collarbone. The policeman was stretchered away with a broken leg to the local hospital, and then presumably discharged to a desk job in the most rural part of France they could find for him.

Who Needs Hands?

Giant cardboard hands (handed out to spectators by race organisers or sponsors) have been known to injure riders as they sped past overexcited crowds lining the route. After Norway's Thor Hushovd had his arm gashed in 2006 by a spectator brandishing one over the barrier during a sprint finish, the lethal hands were finally withdrawn in favour of foam rubber ones.

Gone to the Dogs

It is not uncommon for idiot dog owners to have their dogs off the lead when the race is passing. This usually results in no more than swerving bikes, cursing riders and red-faced idiot dog owners. In the 2007 Tour, however, it was to be the cause of not one, but two, accidents. During stage 8 the German Marcus Burghardt ran into the rear end of a confused Labrador and flew over his handlebars as the front wheel of his bike buckled. The Labrador's backside survived unscathed and unbuckled. A spectator grabbed it (the Labrador, as opposed to the Labrador's backside) before it could do any more damage.

Later in the same Tour, during stage 18, the Frenchman Sandy Casar was part of a four-man breakaway when he hit a dog running across the road, causing both himself and the Belgian Frederik Willems to crash. Casar got back on his bike, notwithstanding as serious a case of 'road rash of the buttock' as you are ever likely to see (I know this because a close-up shot by a motorcycle cameraman revealed the extent of the decimation in glorious technicolour), and went on to win his first ever, and probably his most painful ever, Tour stage.

Wounded Pride

In 2009 Alberto Contador's pride was knocked when the Danish national anthem was played on the Champs-Elysées to celebrate the Spaniard's second Tour victory. The Spanish national anthem, the 'Marcha Real', is only one of two national anthems in the world to have no official lyrics. On this occasion, it had a whole (Danish) choir to sing its non-lyrics.

Smile, You're on TV

During stage 9 in 2011, a French TV car got too close to a breakaway group of riders and, suddenly swerving to avoid a tree at the side of the road, drove at speed into the Spaniard Juan Antonio Flecha, knocking him off his bike and causing the Dutch rider behind, Johnny

Hoogerland, to fly over a ditch and into a barbed-wire fence. Flecha had a swollen elbow and a hole so big in his knee it couldn't be stitched. Hoogerland had thirty-three stitches and ending up bearing a close resemblance to the fence he had been so intimate with. Both men finished the stage and the Tour! The TV car and its occupants were kicked off the remainder of that year's race.

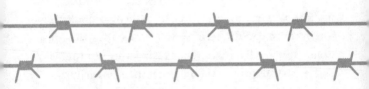

➤ Le Tour Féminin

A women's Tour de France was held on twenty-three occasions between 1984 and 2009. Three women won the race three times: Jeannie Longo of France; Fabiana Luperini of Italy; and Joane Somarriba of Spain. Britain's Nicole Cooke was one of four women to win it twice, and Britain's Emma Pooley won the race the last time it was held in 2009.

The first race in 1984 augured well for the future, with eighteen stages running two to three hours ahead of the men's race each day (but not over the same roads) and millions of spectators lining the routes. But the organisers could never settle into much of a rhythm, given the constant battle they faced to get sufficient sponsorship to run the race. As a result, the race didn't take place at all in 1990, 1991 or 2004, and the routes and the number of stages in other years were determined by which, and how many, cities agreed to contribute funds and host a stage start or finish. By 2009, the race had been reduced to four stages and sixty-six riders.

Variously known as 'La Grande Boucle Féminine', 'Le Tour Féminin' and the 'Tour Cycliste Féminin', the organisers were not even able to settle on a single name for the race, partly because the men's Tour de France organisers rather unchivalrously warned them off using anything that might breach their copyright.

Intermittent cries are still heard for the women's Tour to be reinstated and properly supported, but in the meantime the blue riband race for professional women riders must remain the Giro d'Italia Femminile (known colloquially as the 'Giro Donne').

Chapter 7
Doping and Cheating

'We are completely innocent. We run a very clean and professional team that has been singled out due to our success...'

Lance Armstrong, December 2000

'I'll spend the rest of my life trying to earn back trust and apologise to people...'

Lance Armstrong, January 2013

We will get to Lance Armstrong shortly, I promise, but first let us be clear on a few things. Cheating in its many guises, including doping, has been going on since the first Tour de France in 1903, and literally thousands of riders have been involved in some way, shape or form. Doping had become so acceptable by 1930 that Desgrange felt obliged to remind riders in the rule book that year that drugs were not among the items that would be provided by the organisers, and any system that encourages high rewards and low punishments is going to make cheating irresistible to human beings with less-than-saintly morals. So, sooner or later, punishments had to become, well, punishing. Only then could the weeding process really begin. And begin it eventually did, but not before the 1960s, and not really in earnest until the twenty-first century.

Attitudes to doping in particular have changed dramatically over the decades. This really kicked off when riders started to pay a price of up to and including death for abusing their own bodies, one of the most notable being the British rider Tom Simpson, who, as we have seen, collapsed and died on Mont Ventoux in 1967. They only had to check Tom Simpson's pockets to discover the drugs (amphetamines) that had contributed to his untimely death, but in the decades that followed drugs became increasingly sophisticated and increasingly difficult to detect. Those who doped systematically at a team level comfortably won the so-called 'arms race' by staying a couple of steps ahead of those who tried to catch them out. But medical science was always going to catch up sooner or later and lab technicians began to develop more effective tests. By 2005, they could retrospectively tell, from urine samples taken in 1999, that 10 per cent of the riders tested during the 1999 Tour had at that time taken the performance-enhancing drug EPO (erythropoietin) – and the guilty riders in question included you-know-who.

And then something even more dramatic, but much less technical, happened. As the authorities closed in for another attempt at the kill in 2012, the lid suddenly blew off the hitherto sacrosanct *omertà* of the cycling brotherhood. Doper started outing doper in the hope of securing immunity from prosecution. It was supergrass time. And the level of scandal was to prove so great that it would need Oprah Winfrey to sort it out. But let us first go back to the beginning.

Le président, il dit 'oui'!
(The president, he says 'yes')

On his way to becoming the first rider to win the Tour five times, Frenchman Jacques Anquetil appeared on television a number of times in the early 1960s to argue that doping was essential for painkilling reasons and that it should therefore be a matter of personal choice for riders. The French president at the time, Charles de Gaulle, famously defended him on the grounds that promoting French success abroad was far more important than the 'irrelevant' subject of doping.

All Aboard!

In the second Tour de France in 1904, twelve riders were disqualified for reasons that included jumping on board cars, buses or trains during the night stages that were then a feature of the race. The disqualified riders included the winner, Maurice Garin, who had already won the first-ever Tour the year before. His winning margin in 1903, over the second-shortest course in the history of the race, still stands today as the highest winning margin on record, so it's fairly safe to assume that he travelled in 1903 *and* 1904 with bus and train timetables in his saddlebag.

A Moral Dilemma

There is much evidence that doping was rife throughout the peloton from the very start, but it wasn't actually illegal during the first six decades of the Tour. All the controversy that surrounded it until 1965, when doping became illegal in France, was therefore of a moral nature. But, lest we judge too harshly or too quickly on the morals that prevailed over those six decades, we must recognise that the race organisers over that period showed scant regard for the health or safety of the riders who took part in the Tour de France. Taking 1920 as an example, riders had to complete 5,503 kilometres (3,420 miles) over fifteen stages, with an average stage distance therefore of 367 kilometres (230 miles). The 2012 Tour riders, on much lighter bikes and enjoying all the benefits of twenty-first-century sports science, had to cover a paltry 3,488 kilometres (2,180 miles) over twenty-one stages, with a stage average therefore of 166 kilometres (104 miles). Only twenty-two of the 113 riders who started the race in 1920 were able to finish it. Of the 198 who started in 2012, 153 made it to the end. Little wonder, then, that the earlier riders felt they couldn't even complete the race without drinking brandy, administering chloroform to their gums and rubbing cocaine into their eyes.

Roger and Out

In 1960 the Frenchman Roger Rivière rode over a ravine and broke his back. It was later revealed that he had been unable to apply his brakes because his hands were too numb from the number of painkillers he had taken.

Brains, Muscles, Blood

As the early drugs (ether, strychnine, chloroform, cocaine, amphetamines) stimulated the brain at the same time as deadening the pain, there were downsides. Overexcited riders often launched crazy attacks and used up their energy too soon.

In the 1970s, anabolic steroids (including testosterone) and growth hormones became *les drogues du jour* and, while they strengthened muscles and reduced recovery times, they too had unfortunate side effects. They could make riders heavy and bloated and could therefore drag them down over a long, hot stage race like the Tour.

Clean riders, therefore, felt able to compete with 'brain' or 'muscle' dopers over a three-week period, but that would all change when the focus switched to blood. By the 1990s EPO was being used to stimulate the kidneys to produce more oxygen-carrying red blood cells and this increased the overall performance of world-class athletes by about 5 per cent, which equates in Tour de France terms to the difference between first place and the middle of the pack, to the difference between glory and relative obscurity. The gap between clean and doping riders widened further from 2000 onwards when illegal blood transfusions before and during races enhanced performance yet further (riders' own blood would be taken and stored until it was needed to top up depleted red blood cells during races).

The Festina Affair

Just before the start of the 1998 Tour, Willy Voet, a soigneur of the Festina team, was discovered by customs officials to have a large stash of illegal doping products and paraphernalia in the boot of his car. The

Not for the Faint-hearted

Before the effects of EPO were fully understood
and managed, it is thought that up to a
dozen professional cyclists died when their
hearts stopped under the strain of trying
to pump their EPO-thickened blood.

Festina team was kicked out of the Tour and other
teams left in disgrace or disgust as the Tour progressed
– only ninety-six out of 189 starters finished the race
that year. A succession of police raids, confessions and
trials over the next couple of years led to the inevitable
conclusion that systematic doping at a team level was
prevalent throughout the peloton. Stricter testing
measures were put in place, but individual and team
results continued to improve and eyebrows continued
to be raised.

The Unlevel Level Playing Field

It was often argued by dopers that everybody else
was taking the same performance-enhancing drugs
at the same time, so what's the problem with a level
playing field of dopers? The problem is that different
human bodies react differently to the same latest
doping methods, so having the physiology that just

happens to react most favourably to the *drogue du moment* is not quite the same thing as being the best rider of your generation. And then there's always the added complication of having some riders who are determined at all costs not to cheat. Inconvenient, that.

A 'Passing' Acquaintance

The Belgian rider Michel Pollentier was caught trying to fool the testers in 1978 when he attempted to provide a sample from a condom filled with someone else's urine. I'm not sure how close a friend you have to be to loan somebody your urine, but certainly more than just a 'passing' acquaintance, I would have thought.

It's Much Easier when You're on Drugs

It isn't, you know. It's hard enough to ride *pan y agua* (Spanish for 'bread and water' i.e. 'clean'), but it's even harder to ride full of chemicals and freshly topped-up blood. This is because doped riders have constant opportunities to ride through higher and higher levels of pain. When you can taste blood in your mouth, when your muscles are screaming and when your heart feels like it's about to explode, the drugs and the fresh blood will allow you to keep going, but only if you're hard enough to take the extra pain that comes with it. Professional cyclists have very high thresholds of pain. Doping professional cyclists need to develop higher thresholds still. The drugs work, but they hurt.

The 'Arms Race'

The anti-doping authorities continued to enjoy some success in the first decade of the new century. They stripped American Floyd Landis of the 2006 title after he tested positive for testosterone, and they suspended a number of big-name riders that same year after a drugs bust linked them to the dodgy Spanish doctor Eufamiano Fuentes. The following year they kicked out one of the race favourites, the Kazakh Alexandre Vinokourov (after he was found to have been blood-doping), and the wearer at the time of the yellow jersey, the Dane Michael Rasmussen (after he was found to have lied about his whereabouts when he missed earlier doping tests). They introduced individual 'biological passports' in 2008, so that blood test results could subsequently be measured against a rider's base blood levels. They stripped the Spaniard Alberto Contador of the 2010 title after he tested positive for the performance-enhancing drug clenbuterol. By 2010, half the winners of the Tour since 1980 had either admitted doping or tested positive.

The Tour's 'Ashes'

In 2007, sickened by the Tour's most recent doping scandals, the newspaper *France Soir* devoted its entire front page to a mock obituary, stating that the Tour had sadly died, at the age of 104, as a result of a long illness. The paper went on to say that the funeral would be held in a strictly private circle. This was a parody of the 1882 article in *The Sporting Times* (after Australia had beaten England at the Oval for the first time), which announced the death of English cricket and advised that the body would be cremated and the ashes taken to Australia, hence the need ever since to regain/retain 'the Ashes'.

Lance Armstrong

Throughout the years that followed the Festina affair, one man had continued to rack up a record-breaking number of titles, had continued to test negative, and had continued to pour scorn on the detractors who wouldn't believe he was clean. That man was Lance Armstrong, an iconic sporting superhero for the new century. Or not.

If you wanted to say some kind things about Lance Armstrong, you could point out that he showed great bravery in recovering from life-threatening cancer, that he raised millions of dollars for his Livestrong charity, that he inspired a generation of American kids to try that bit harder, and that he seems to be at least a bit sorry now for what he did. And, anyway, isn't he just one of dozens of loveable rogues who have been driven to win at all costs? Jacques Anquetil took drugs and remains revered, cycling fans still think fondly of Tom Simpson, Alberto Contador remains a hero, at least within Spain, and you can't help but laugh at that cheeky Maurice Garin for jumping on trains in the middle of a night-time stage.

So why is Lance Armstrong so reviled in comparison with other drug-takers and cheats? Is it because he won more times than any other rider by foul means, and got richer than any other rider as a result? Is it because so many people knew he was a cheat all along but just couldn't prove it? Is it because he bullied, ridiculed and sued so many of his detractors on the way up that there now is a long queue of people waiting to kick him even harder on the way down? Is it because the testimonies of eleven former teammates to the United States Anti-Doping Agency (USADA) and, in particular, Tyler Hamilton's 2012 book *The Secret Race*, have laid bare the extent of his cheating in such gory detail? Is it because he gave such a maudlin, unconvincing performance throughout the 2012 Oprah Winfrey interview? It is, of course, for all of those reasons. But what did he actually do?

By his own admission, he enhanced his Tour de France performances through the use of EPO, cortisone, testosterone, human growth hormones, steroids and blood transfusions. He went to extraordinary lengths to avoid detection and became an expert on the 'glow time' of the illegal substances he used ('glow time' is the number of hours that substances can be detected in the body after they have been taken, during which time the cyclist needs to avoid a meeting with a dope tester). He coerced many of his fellow riders on the US Postal and Discovery Channel teams to take the same illegal substances he took himself. He publicly vilified those who dared to accuse him of cheating, including *Sunday Times* journalist David Walsh and Betsy Andreu, the wife of former teammate, Frankie Andreu. He reportedly bullied clean riders to keep their mouths shut and sold out fellow riders to the doping authorities if they dared to perform better on the same performance-enhancing drugs he himself was taking. Sympathy is going to be hard to find on the way down.

Let Down by a Generation

We must remember still that doping within professional cycling has been a widespread problem for a very long time. Tyler Hamilton has referred to the 'dark period of cycling that we all went through'. When Bradley Wiggins was asked whether he felt let down by Lance

Armstrong, he replied that he didn't, because so many cyclists were doing it back then: 'Rather than feel let down by him, I think that whole generation let us down.'

The problem still hasn't gone away. The Luxembourger Frank Schleck was kicked out of the 2012 Tour after showing positive for the illegal diuretic xipamide, illegal because it acts as a masking agent, i.e. it dilutes urine to the extent that other substances don't show up. But testing has become more effective and the number of positive tests is reducing. Only 2 per cent of lab tests in 2011 discovered newly formed red blood cells, i.e. signs of EPO use or blood transfusions. The figure in 2001 had been 11 per cent. The winning time up l'Alpe d'Huez in 2011 was 41 minutes 21 seconds. That same time in 2001 would have earned you fortieth place for the climb. And the sport's governing body, the UCI (Union Cycliste Internationale) looks as if it might finally be falling into line with the stricter regimes of the world and Olympic anti-doping agencies.

The Brailsford Effect

Perhaps even more significant for the future well-being of the sport is the proof positive provided by Dave Brailsford and his team in recent times that *clean* success can be achieved through hard work, nth degree planning and incremental improvements across the board. At the 2008 Beijing Games, Brailsford led the most dominant Olympic performance ever seen by a single team, and it was, furthermore, a team from one of the great backwaters of cycling, i.e. Great Britain. That was track cycling, so he had yet to prove that the same could be achieved in the world of road racing. So he took charge of the Sky Procycling team and did it all over again, sweeping up first and second spots on the podium in the 2012 Tour de France, along with a total of six stage wins by three different riders.

Chapter 8
The Legacy of the Tour

Hopefully you have enjoyed looking back over the history of the greatest bike race on earth and you are looking forward to many more great Tours in the years ahead.

Some things are probably not going to change that much. It's always going to be quite a French affair, for one thing, and the organisers are unlikely to try and better the Champs-Elysées as a finishing straight any time soon. There are still going to be heroic climbs, exciting sprint finishes and edge-of-the-seat time trials. There will be coloured jerseys and huge sums of money as prizes. Glamour, hype, speed and danger will combine to provide the same heady mix that we just can't get enough of once a year in the French summer.

Some things that have always changed will continue to change. The routes, for one thing. Each year will mix old favourites like l'Alpe d'Huez, Mont Ventoux or the Promenade des Anglais with brand new stages like Corsica or Yorkshire! Even the Emir of Qatar has expressed an interest in hosting a prologue. (Money is presumably no object but distance from Paris and temperatures of 50 degrees centigrade most certainly are).

Bikes will become increasingly space-age, but they will still have two wheels and a saddle and they will still have to be pedalled hard around France for three weeks.

And some things will simply take us by surprise, even shock us. Young exciting riders will come through to challenge the older legs, crashes will end careers, cheats that we never suspected of being cheats will be caught cheating, and cheats that we did suspect of cheating may finally confess their sins and beg our forgiveness. Some might even mean it.

The sport of cycling has gone global in the twenty-first century, but the Tour de France continues to stand apart as the most famous, most anticipated and most exciting bicycle race in the world. It will prevail because it remains far bigger than any individual rider or team, than any particular stage or year, than all the scientific and medical developments that tinker at it edges. Long may it continue to thrill us. *Vive le Tour de France!*

About the Author

Ray Hamilton is a freelance writer and editor, whose lifelong passions are sport, travel, languages and history. If ever those four passions were wrapped up in a single subject, that subject must surely be the Tour de France, so it is perhaps unsurprising that it has become his favourite sporting event, and the subject of this, his second book.

He has edited books on a wide range of subjects and previously pursued a varied career in government, the highlights of which included multilateral government negotiations in Paris and forays into sub-Saharan Africa.

Acknowledgements

My thanks go to all at Summersdale who have supported the production of this book, and in particular to Chris Turton for his excellent editorial steering and guidance. His knowledge of all things cycling remains streets ahead of my own. Thanks also to Caroline Hodgson for her eagle-eyed copy-editing.

RAY HAMILTON

The Joy of Cycling

Ray Hamilton

ISBN: 978 1 84953 457 4   Hardback   £9.99

*'Be at one with the Universe. If you can't
do that, at least be at one with you bike'*

LENNARD ZINN

This pocket-sized miscellany, packed with fascinating
facts, handy hints and captivating stories and quotes
from the world of cycling, is perfect for anyone who
knows the incomparable joy of bikes.

JOHN O'GROATS

mud

sweat&

GEARS

CYCLING FROM LAND'S END
TO JOHN O'GROATS (VIA THE PUB)

LAND'S END

ellie bennett

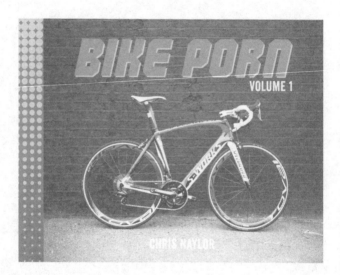

If you're interested in finding out more about
our books, find us on Facebook at
Summersdale Publishers
and follow us on Twitter at
@Summersdale.

www.summersdale.com